Addressing Stress With Self-Compassion

A Guide for Early Childhood Teachers

David P. Barry

Foreword by Kristin Neff

TEACHERS COLLEGE PRESS
TEACHERS COLLEGE | COLUMBIA UNIVERSITY
NEW YORK AND LONDON

This book is a reimagining of the author's dissertation. As such, it utilizes direct and reworked content (e.g., references, data, excerpts, etc.) from that dissertation (Barry, 2021). The dissertation study was funded in part by the University of Texas at Austin's College of Education Graduate Student Research Award.

Published by Teachers College Press,® 1234 Amsterdam Avenue, New York, NY 10027

Copyright © 2024 by David P. Barry

Front cover design by Holly Grundon / BHG Graphics. Illustration by BRO Vector / iStock by Getty Images.

All rights reserved. No part of this publication may be reproduced or transmitted in any form or by any means, electronic or mechanical, including photocopy, or any information storage and retrieval system, without permission from the publisher. For reprint permission and other subsidiary rights requests, please contact Teachers College Press, Rights Dept.: tcpressrights@tc.columbia.edu

Library of Congress Cataloging-in-Publication Data is available at loc.gov

ISBN 978-0-8077-6984-3 (paper)
ISBN 978-0-8077-6985-0 (hardcover)
ISBN 978-0-8077-8246-0 (ebook)

Printed on acid-free paper
Manufactured in the United States of America

I dedicate this book to the participants who so generously shared of themselves to inform the content of this book. May your words inspire new, preservice, and veteran early childhood teachers everywhere to care for themselves with self-compassion.

Contents

Foreword *Kristin Neff*		xi
Acknowledgments		xiii
Introduction		1
	Repeat After Me: I Am Not Supposed to Be Good at This Yet!	1
1.	**Making an Empirical Case for Self-Compassion Practice in Preservice Teacher Education Programs**	8
	Why I Was Burning Out	8
	Preservice Teachers' Experiences With Stress	10
	Scholarship Aimed at Addressing Preservice Teachers' Well-Being	12
	Self-Compassion: A Potential Way Forward	14
	Scholarly Attempts at Reducing Stress Among Preservice Early Childhood Teachers	17
2.	**My Mixed-Methods Case Study: The Impact of Self-Compassion Practice on Preservice Teachers**	22
	Recruiting Participants and Data Collection	23
	Findings: Self-Compassion Practice Mattered to These Preservice Teachers	28
3.	**The Stress of Delivering Academic Content to Students**	56
	My Own Challenges Delivering Academic Content as a Preservice Teacher	57
	Why Is Delivering Academic Content to Students Stressful for Preservice Teachers?	58

Addressing the Stress of Delivering Academic Content to
Students With Self-Compassion 68

4. **The Stress of Meeting Students' Social, Emotional, and Behavioral Needs** 79

    My Own Challenges Meeting Students' Social, Emotional,
    and Behavioral Needs 81

    Why Is Meeting Students' Social, Emotional, and Behavioral
    Needs Stressful for Preservice Teachers? 81

    Addressing the Stress of Meeting Students' Social, Emotional,
    and Behavioral Needs With Self-Compassion 90

5. **The Stress of Relationship Dynamics With Cooperating Teachers, School Staff, Families, and Teacher Educators** 97

    My Own Challenges Managing Relationship Dynamics With
    Cooperating Teachers, School Staff, Families, and
    Teacher Educators 97

    Why Are Relationship Dynamics With Cooperating Teachers,
    School Staff, Families, and Teacher Educators Stressful for
    Preservice Teachers? 98

    Addressing the Stress of Managing Relationship Dynamics With
    Cooperating Teachers, School Staff, Families, and Teacher
    Educators With Self-Compassion 111

6. **The Stress of Life Outside the Classroom** 119

    Why Is Balancing Life Outside the Classroom Stressful for
    Preservice Teachers? 120

    Addressing the Stress of Life Outside the Classroom With
    Self-Compassion 122

7. **Moving Forward With Self-Compassion: A Call for Stakeholders to Take Action** 128

    Scholarly Significance of Self-Compassionate Letter-Writing
    With Preservice Teachers 129

    Implications for Early Childhood Stakeholders 130

Appendix A: Self-Compassion Scale—Short Form (SCS-SF) (Raes et al., 2011)   **135**

Appendix B: Participant Information and Statistical Tests   **137**

References   **143**

Index   **149**

About the Author   **153**

Foreword

Being a teacher has never been easy, and it seems that with every new generation of teachers, novel challenges present themselves. Teachers deal with an incredible amount of stress: low pay, excessive paperwork, high-need students, not to mention school shootings. Those who muscle through this stress are lauded for being "superheroes." But teachers aren't superheroes—they aren't invincible, and they aren't made of steel. Teachers are human beings, and as humans, they have limits on what they can withstand.

In this book, you'll learn about the wide range of challenges, stressors, joys, and excitements that go along with becoming and being an early childhood teacher. The author of this book (a former student of mine) also adds in sage advice about how self-compassion can make this journey a bit easier. The word *compassion* is derived from Latin and refers to how we're with (com) our suffering (passion). It involves treating yourself with the same kindness, care, warmth, and support when you're struggling that you'd naturally show to a close friend or colleague.

You might not be convinced that self-compassion is such a good thing. Won't it make me soft or weak, you might wonder? Research shows that self-compassion is one of the most powerful sources of strength, coping, and resilience you can have as a teacher. When you're in the battle of life—and let's face it, being a teacher often feels like a battle—what's going to make you stronger? Being an ally to yourself, encouraging and supporting yourself, or being an enemy to yourself, shaming and undermining yourself? Having your own back will help you get through the challenges of being a teacher much more effectively than giving yourself the cold shoulder.

But isn't it selfish? Shouldn't all my compassion be aimed toward my students? The truth is, the more compassion flows inward to yourself, the more resources you'll have available to give to your kids. And research shows that self-compassion will reduce your level of burnout so you can keep on giving.

But won't it make me lazy and unmotivated? In fact, research shows that self-compassion is a much more effective motivator than harsh self-criticism. Imagine if you tried to motivate a student who was struggling the way we often motivate ourselves. "I'm ashamed of you. You're a worthless loser who'll never amount to anything. You better improve or else!" You would never say such a thing to a student because you know the negative effect it would have. Well, this cruel inner dialogue has the same impact on you. Relentless self-criticism creates fear of failure, and performance anxiety and undermines self-confidence. When we fail and shame ourselves for being a failure, it makes it harder for us to learn from our setbacks. Constructive criticism that is warm and encouraging is more effective at creating the learning and growth orientation needed to learn from our mistakes and grow from them. That's why it's so important to treat ourselves with the same compassion we naturally show to others.

It's my sincere hope that you can learn to have compassion for the challenges of being an early childhood teacher and support yourself with kindness when you inevitably stumble. I also hope that you can appreciate yourself and all the good you do for the world. You don't have to earn the right to compassion, all you need to be is a flawed and imperfect human being. By embracing your humanity and opening your heart to yourself, not only will you find inner strength, you will also be a wonderful role model to your colleagues and young students.

Dr. Kristin Neff, PhD
Associate Professor of Human Development and Culture
Educational Psychology Department
University of Texas at Austin

Acknowledgments

There are so many people I want to thank for their support over the years who helped make this book a possibility. I wish to thank my dissertation committee: Christopher P. Brown, Allison Skerrett, Catherine Riegle-Crumb, Kristin Neff, and Maleka Donaldson. Your support and encouragement continue to mean more than I can express. Sarah Jubar, you are a literal dream come true, and I sing your praises as an editor at every opportunity.

My family and friends who remind me that I'm not an imposter when I feel like one: you encourage me to be kinder to myself. Steve and Mabel: Thank you for helping me stay grounded when I start teetering into a spiral; you encourage me to be more mindful. My JQS family who taught me how to be a teacher and my WCU family: you encourage my sense of common humanity by being a consistent reminder that I am—and always will be—part of a community of educators.

Addressing Stress With Self-Compassion

Introduction

REPEAT AFTER ME: I AM NOT SUPPOSED TO BE GOOD AT THIS YET!

To begin, I want to congratulate you and thank you for making the decision to become a teacher. Whether you are getting started on your teaching certification, already have some experience working in schools, or are early on in your career as a classroom teacher, your journey will be incredibly rewarding, challenging, stressful, exciting, and everything in between. At times, you will be so overwhelmed by the process of learning to teach that you may lose sight of the enormity of the positive impact you're making on the lives of the young children you are working with; you might feel like quitting. At other times, you'll be just as overwhelmed by the joy, wonder, brilliance, and humor your students bring to the classroom every day, reminding you of why you made the decision to become a teacher in the first place. In my 12 years as a preschool and kindergarten teacher and in my 4 years of preservice early childhood teacher education in college, I felt the full range of these emotions—sometimes simultaneously! Now that I've become an early childhood teacher educator, I feel I have an obligation to share what I learned along the way when it comes to the challenges I experienced on my own journey becoming a teacher and what I've learned from the preservice early childhood teachers I have supported in becoming teachers over the last several years. I wrote this book to do just that.

Before you get too far into this book, I want to share with you a few things about learning to become a teacher that I wish someone had told me before I started student teaching. First and foremost—*you aren't supposed to be good at this yet*. Anyone who is making you feel that you should have perfect lesson plans or that your classroom management should be airtight or that the line of children you're walking down the hallway should be straight and silent has either never been an early childhood teacher or has forgotten what it was like to be responsible for a classroom full of young children. If the person making you feel that you should already be an excellent and effective teacher is *you*, this is the book for you. Know this: If teaching were something that people were good at right away, there would be no reason for teacher education programs, mentoring programs, or the gift of time and experience. Like any skill or craft, learning to be an effective teacher takes time (Darling-Hammond, 2000; Fantilli & McDougall, 2009).

Do you remember when you got your learner's permit and drove for the first time? How did it go? If it was anything like my first time behind the wheel, it wasn't great. There were so many small details I had to learn to pay attention to at the same time: my mirrors, my blind spot, where the gas and brake were, how fast I was going, remembering to signal, looking out for other cars and pedestrians—the list goes on. At that time, coordinating all of those small but critical pieces into a connected driving experience felt impossible. After lots of practice and experience driving—and a few narrowly avoided mishaps—it feels like second nature; it's something I can just do. It feels automatic.

For me, and for most of my teacher friends, learning to teach young children was very similar to learning to drive a car: so many small but critical components that needed to be coordinated in a cohesive way but at first felt impossible to do well. I could plan a great lesson and go through all the detailed steps I'd planned, but how could I do that while *also* making sure the children were engaged? What would happen when they'd asked a question I couldn't answer? What if someone vomited in the middle of my read-aloud? And, oh my, did they sometimes vomit—and sometimes that vomit triggered a domino effect of more vomit. Should I keep reading? How could I get everyone's attention at the same time, get them lined up quietly, and remember who the line leader and door holder were and get them to gym silently and in a straight line without losing anyone along the way? Inevitably, someone's shoe would come untied going up the staircase, and I'd have to stop everyone so I could tie it while another class was coming down the staircase at the same time—and of course their line was silent, straight, and everyone's shoes were tied. Meanwhile, I'd be doing everything I could to not fall backwards down the stairs while two children started arguing about which of them was a faster runner or who got more money from the tooth fairy.

After years—and I do mean *years*—of being a kindergarten teacher, I learned how to anticipate and juggle all the things needed to be an effective teacher. I don't say this to scare you away from teaching. On the contrary, I say it to encourage you and to remind you that becoming an effective teacher takes a long time and lots of mistakes.

In all honesty, it wasn't until probably my 7th year of being a teacher that I felt like I could manage it all without agonizing over every detail. Around that 7th year, knowing what to do in a given situation was finally something that felt like an automatic response—like driving a car. That's not to say that I didn't have fantastic experiences working with children and families while I was student teaching or in those first few years; I absolutely did. It also doesn't mean that I didn't get the occasional curveball in my 12th year of teaching; that certainly happened, too. What it means is that with time, experience, lots of mistakes, and lots of triumphs, I finally started to feel like I knew what I was doing and that I was doing it well. Research actually backs this up: The teachers who have the greatest impact on student achievement are those who have the most teaching experience (Darling-Hammond, 2000; Fantilli & McDougall, 2009). With that in mind, I want you to read this phrase out loud and repeat it to yourself whenever anyone—including you—makes you feel that you are supposed to be an expert the moment you begin student teaching. Ready? Here goes: *I am not supposed to be good at this yet; it takes a long time to become a good teacher.*

Take a deep breath, look at yourself in the mirror, and repeat: *I am not supposed to be good at this yet; it takes a long time to become a good teacher.*

With that sentiment in mind and that commitment to accepting that you are learning how to be a teacher—and will be learning how to be a good teacher for a long time—read on to learn more about how this book will be helpful to you on your journey. Congratulations on making one of the best decisions you will ever make, and thank you for your commitment to the children you will meet as a student teacher and the future children you will meet as a classroom teacher. You are all fortunate to have each other!

The Purpose of This Book

There hasn't been much research on the stressors experienced specifically by preservice early childhood teachers (e.g., Hirshberg, 2017; Horgan et al., 2018). That said, there are a few things teacher educators and researchers do know about these stressors and challenges. First of all, learning how to teach is stressful (Horgan et al., 2018). In fact, the coping mechanisms you develop as a student teacher are likely to be the coping mechanisms you will use to handle stress as a classroom teacher (Horgan et al., 2018). Research is beginning to include stress as one of the likely reasons that nearly 40–50% of teachers leave teaching within the first 5 years (Djonko-Moore, 2016; Ryan et al., 2017). Learning to manage the inevitable challenges you will face as a developing teacher in a healthy way is therefore of the utmost importance.

Second, you are living in multiple worlds right now; you are a student, you are a teacher, and you are all of the other brilliant, wonderful, and complex "things" you are. Navigating these multiple worlds is challenging, and balancing them successfully will depend on several factors:

- Does your cooperating teacher treat you like a student, another teacher, or something in between?
- Do your students treat you like a friend or a teacher?
- Does being a student mean that you are working to pay for school in addition to taking classes and student teaching?

- Do your professors, bosses, supervisors, and cooperating teachers understand the balancing act you are performing?
- Are you engaged with things outside of school, work, and student teaching, like your family, friends, hobbies, and interests?

Taken together, the answers to these questions paint a complex picture of what being a student teacher will be like for you; being stressed is likely inevitable.

Early childhood teacher educators and researchers like me also recognize that there is a lot more to know about how we can be supportive to you as you navigate the challenges, joys, and stressors of learning to become a teacher. To date, there have been very few studies aimed at understanding and addressing those challenges and stressors that preservice early childhood teachers deal with while enrolled in teacher education programs (Beltman et al., 2011; Hirshberg, 2017; Horgan et al., 2018). Given that there is so much we don't know, it feels critical to share with you what we *do* know; that is where this book comes in.

This book uncovers the typical and specific challenges experienced by many preservice early childhood teachers (ranging from challenges with classroom management to balancing coursework and fieldwork expectations with their personal lives) throughout their teacher education. Knowing what these challenges are ahead of time and realizing that you are not the only preservice teacher to experience them is one of the first steps toward make your journey of becoming a teacher less stressful—knowing you are not alone.

Throughout the book, I share insights from a range of preservice early childhood teachers who experienced these same challenges and how they addressed and managed them throughout their teacher education and into their first year of teaching. These challenges and how they responded to them with self-compassion come from my analysis of data collected from a 2-year longitudinal, mixed-methods case study in which I followed a diverse cohort of preservice early childhood teachers ($n = 16$) from their first semester of student teaching and into their first year of teaching (Barry, 2021).

Over the course of this study, I learned a great deal as an early childhood teacher educator and researcher about the myriad of factors that make learning to be a teacher stressful. Though I learned that the challenges are many, I also learned that they are not uncommon; many of the preservice teachers had very similar experiences with stress while learning to become teachers. Additionally, through a deliberate practice of addressing the challenges with self-compassion—more on that in a moment—they learned to respond to their stress with a combined sense of mindfulness, being kinder to themselves, and the developing realization that they were not alone in their experience of stress—that "not being good at this yet" was normal (Barry, 2021, 2022).

To help you with this process of managing the challenges of becoming an excellent teacher, I explain how to address the specific stressors you will likely experience throughout your training and induction with self-compassion. Dr. Kristin Neff defines self-compassion as three interacting components: mindfulness, self-kindness, and a sense of common humanity. In its simplest terms, being self-compassionate is treating yourself and speaking to yourself just as you would to someone you love and reminding yourself that all people experience challenges and make mistakes (Neff, 2011; Neff & Germer, 2013). That said, its meaning becomes more powerful when you experience it firsthand.

Think about a mistake you made recently. What words and feelings come to mind when you think about that mistake? Really take a moment to pause here; maybe even write some of the words down that come to mind. When I think about some of my early teaching mistakes, the words that come to mind are pretty harsh: idiot, incompetent, bad teacher, unworthy, terrible, and so on. Now, imagine someone you love made the exact same mistake you just paused to think about; what words and phrases would you say to them about it? Take another moment to pause here and write down some of those words and phrases. Are they similar? Different? (based on a self-compassion exercise by Neff, 2011). When I think back to those early teaching mistakes and what I would say to a loved one who'd made the same mistake, the words and phrases that come to mind are very different. Phrases like "That must have been really hard," or "I'm so sorry that happened," or "Try to see this as a learning opportunity. What could you do differently next time?" are what come to my mind.

You may have read that last paragraph and think self-compassion is about letting yourself off the hook for "bad" behavior. This couldn't be further from the truth (Neff & Germer, 2018). To be self-compassionate requires an awareness of the reality of a situation (i.e., mindfulness)—if something you are doing is unhealthy for you, pretending like everything is fine when it isn't wouldn't be self-compassionate; it would be self-destructive. When we truly love someone, it's unlikely that we would encourage them to continue to engage in self-destructive behavior. Rather, we would try to help this person we love see how their actions were harming them and offer them compassion as they work toward changing the negative patterns in their lives. To be self-compassionate, therefore, requires us to always have our best interests and our overall wellness in mind (Neff & Germer, 2018).

The preservice and first-year early childhood teachers whose voices are shared in this book engaged in formal self-compassion practices throughout their student teaching experience. Their voices come from interviews, journals they kept, and self-compassionate letters they wrote themselves as they navigated the challenges of learning to become teachers that I collected and analyzed for the dissertation study on which this book is based (Barry,

2021). It is my sincerest hope that the kindness they offer themselves in the letters and the connections you feel to their challenges will inspire you to be kinder to yourself and feel more connected to all the new and developing teachers out there who may be—and likely are—feeling the same way that you do.

Finally, throughout this book, I provide you with numerous opportunities to engage in self-compassion practices that are tailored to the specific challenges you will likely experience throughout your teacher education program. Research demonstrates that practicing self-compassion increases self-compassion (e.g., Neff & Germer, 2013). Further, heightened levels of self-compassion are associated with fewer instances of job-related stress and burnout and increases in job satisfaction (e.g., Barnard & Curry, 2012; Shapiro et al., 2005). In fact, the preservice teachers from the study guiding this book experienced a significant increase in overall self-compassion from the beginning to the end of their enrollment in the teacher education program (Barry, 2021, 2022, 2023). Taken together, learning to be self-compassionate as you learn to be a teacher holds promise for making learning to be a teacher less stressful.

Furthermore, if you use this book and its self-compassion practices to manage your stress as you learn to become a teacher, it is likely that you will become a teacher who manages stress with self-compassion (Horgan et al., 2018), so why not learn to manage all of it with self-compassion?

How to Use This Book

I designed this book to combine theory, research, and practice in a way that highlights common stressors experienced by early childhood preservice teachers, sharing how the preservice early childhood teachers from my dissertation study reframed those stressors with self-compassion, and offering you the opportunity to practice doing so, too. Each chapter begins with vignettes from my own student teaching experience and into my first year of teaching about challenges I experienced and mistakes I made. Then each chapter explores how my participants experienced those stressors so you can anticipate them and be more prepared to manage them. I hope you are inspired by these vignettes and stories to reframe some of the feelings of inadequacy you may be experiencing as a developing teacher with self-compassion as they did.

At the end of each chapter, I've written self-compassion prompts aimed at addressing the specific challenges and stressors in that chapter. Take the opportunity to engage in these practices so that you too may experience the benefits of self-compassion. Finally, you will be prompted throughout this book to rate your self-compassion on Neff's Self-Compassion Scale—Short Form (Raes et al., 2011) (see Appendix A). If you are like the preservice early childhood teachers I worked with to create this book, you will likely see a significant increase in your self-compassion, which, as stated earlier, has been linked to fewer instances of work-related stress and greater instances of job satisfaction (Barnard & Curry, 2012; Barry, 2021, 2023; Neff & Germer, 2018; Shapiro et al., 2005).

> Note that some of the challenges and stressors you will inevitably experience as a new or developing teacher may need more than self-compassion to work through. If you are finding yourself completely overwhelmed, I can't emphasize enough how helpful it can be to seek out the support of a professional counselor. If you are in college, reach out to the counseling center. If you are already teaching in your own classroom, make an appointment with a mental health counselor. Technology has come a long way since I was in college, and many counselors use telehealth and other online conferencing software to hold therapy sessions with clients. In the last year of my doctoral program, I was teaching pre-K, writing my dissertation, seeing a mental health counselor on Zoom weekly, and writing a self-compassionate letter each day. I believe the combination of counseling from a trained professional and addressing the stressors I was experiencing as a graduate student with self-compassion was what made it possible for me to make it through and graduate. Help is there if you need it, so reach out.

Let's Get Started on Your Journey

You have so much ahead of you on your journey of becoming a teacher—beautiful things, hard things, scary things, hilarious things. Through all of it—the good, the bad, and the ugly—I want you to remember three things. First, that you are not alone; you are connected. Let this book be a reminder to you that what you are experiencing does not need to isolate you; instead, try to let it connect you to all of the other new and developing teachers who came before you who felt that way, as well as those who feel the same way now. Second, you are worthy and deserving of the same kindness you show the people in your life who you love, including your students. When you feel yourself getting self-critical about a child not listening to you or making a mistake when you're teaching, try to address those experiences with kindness and remind yourself of the mantra I gave you at the beginning of this book, which also happens to be the third thing I want you to remember: *You are not supposed to be good at this yet!* Return to this mantra whenever you are doubting yourself. Write it on sticky notes and put them on your mirror and mumble the words to yourself while you're brushing your teeth; *I am not supposed to be good at this yet! It takes a long time to become a good teacher.*

CHAPTER 1

Making an Empirical Case for Self-Compassion Practice in Preservice Teacher Education Programs

I entered my kindergarten classroom in the Boston Public Schools in August 2007 with the intention of staying a kindergarten teacher forever. I entered that room with 4 years of coursework and early childhood classroom experiences that prepared me to teach the content young children needed to know and to deliver that content in ways that were engaging and attended to their sociocultural realities. I entered that room with the intention of earning the trust of my principal, my team, my students, and their families, and did so successfully that year and every year for a decade. By my 10th year, I was earning over $90,000 and was trusted to do what I felt was best for my students by my administration, my students, and their families. I did not fit the mold of a teacher who was burning out, but I was. What I desperately needed and had not entered that room with was the capacity to protect myself from the stress and eventual burnout I felt from being a caregiver to 22 young children year after year. The effects were gradual and manifested as exhaustion, weight gain and loss, and the unrelenting feeling that whatever I did to support my students was never enough.

WHY I WAS BURNING OUT

Year after year, my ability to handle the burnout I was experiencing in healthy ways waned, and my patience for my students dwindled as the emotional exhaustion I was feeling began to take over. The community violence my students witnessed, the food insecurity some of them experienced, and in the direst of situations, the neglect and abuse they revealed to me through disclosures became harder and harder for me to cope with. The new assessments and reforms we had to incorporate and administer year after year left me jaded about being a teacher altogether. I began taking antidepressants and seeing a counselor, which helped to a point. However, the omnipresent recommendation to "practice self-care" began to frustrate me. When, I wondered, could I practice self-care? With 44 shoes to tie, 15 scraped knees to put Band-aids on, 66 assessments to complete by 3:15, and 22 kindergarteners that I could not leave alone, when could I practice self-care? Now that I have been out of my kindergarten classroom for several years, I can appreciate the good intentions behind the encouragement to practice self-care. Moreover, it took leaving my kindergarten classroom to pursue my doctorate to realize that all I had going for me as a teacher did not matter if being a teacher was not sustainable.

Pursuing My Doctorate With a Clear Mission

Not wanting other teachers to experience what I did, I decided to pursue a research agenda that examined and addressed teachers' stress that is leading to their attrition so they could stay in their classrooms in healthy and sustainable ways. All children deserve fantastic teachers; however, many teachers are not prepared to manage the stress that comes along with being fantastic (Fantilli & McDougall, 2009; Ryan et al., 2017). Even prior to the COVID-19 pandemic, in the United States, teachers were leaving the classroom at an alarming rate (8% every year), double that of "high performing countries like Finland and Singapore," with teachers' unique stress being cited as a likely cause (Westervelt, 2016).

Since the COVID-19 pandemic, turnover rates increased nationally to about 10% in the 2021–2022 school year (Diliberti & Schwartz, 2023) and to "around 12–14 percent . . . in urban districts, high-poverty districts, and districts serving predominantly students of color" (Diliberti & Schwartz, 2023, p. 1). Although teacher turnover has historically disproportionately impacted low-income children of color in urban districts when compared to White, suburban, middle- and upper-income areas (Djonko-Moore, 2016), this unfortunate trend has clearly continued post-pandemic (Diliberti & Schwartz, 2023). Such high rates of teacher turnover that continue to rise present serious challenges to school districts and students.

My first semester of doctoral studies helped me to discover how I would address this issue when I took a class on self-compassion. Caring for ourselves the way we care for others is the basis of self-compassion (Neff, 2003), and if I had entered my classroom 10 years before with that ability, I believe I could have stayed a kindergarten teacher forever as planned.

As a developing teacher educator, I have witnessed firsthand how much the preservice teachers I work with suffer as a result of overwhelming feelings of failure and inadequacy. I find myself deeply disheartened by how harsh and critical they can be with themselves and horrified at the experiences of racism they and their students suffer in their courses and field placements. To generalize that how they perceive and respond to the stressors in these spaces and how to support them through those experiences would not adequately address how nuanced each of their experiences has been and is worthy of deep empirical investigation. For these reasons and more, my dissertation was aimed at investigating just that. What follows is a short introduction to how I did this work.

PRESERVICE TEACHERS' EXPERIENCES WITH STRESS

A review of the literature on preservice teachers' experience with stress indicated a severe "paucity of research" relying heavily on self-reported data (Horgan et al., 2018, p. 217); the majority of which is over 15 years old. Horgan et al. (2018) wrote,

> Sources of preservice teacher stress have been reported to derive from behaviour management, workload, and lack of support during school placement (Chaplain, 2008), role conflict, time commitments and a need for occupational mobility (Zimmerman et al., 2008), bullying (Maguire, 2001) and professional demands such as time management, funding, technology, resources . . . administrative and collegiate support, managing a crowded curriculum and examinations. (Facchinetti, 2010, pp. 217–218)

These stressors experienced by preservice teachers closely mirror the stressors that have led to burnout (Chang, 2009; Kelly & Berthelsen, 1995; Wrobel, 2013; Yong & Yue, 2007) and reasons for attrition reported by inservice teachers (Ingersoll, 2001; Ingersoll & Connor, 2009). Important to note, however, is that "[i]t is during initial teacher education that teachers begin to establish adaptive or maladaptive coping skills for dealing with the stress of teaching" and that "relatively little attention has been given to stress management for student teachers" (Horgan et al., 2018, p. 218).

One such study of two cohorts of Australian preservice teachers by Murray-Harvey et al. (2000) found a significant reduction in stress over time from the first semester to the second semester of field placement. Further, students who felt they could seek support from their cooperating teachers as a result of a perceived positive relationship consistently reported lower levels of stress (Murray-Harvey et al., 2000). However, when the bond between preservice teacher and cooperating teacher was not as strong, preservice teachers experienced more stress and received a "poorer rating of the[ir] . . . teaching performance" (p. 32).

An additional source of stress may be the disconnect preservice teachers feel when they "have broad theoretical knowledge but are challenged when faced with real situations" (Onchwari, 2010, p. 392). Onchwari (2010) synthesized empirical literature by such scholars as Darling-Hammond et al. (2000), Early & Winton (2001), and McCann & Johannessen (2004) to deduce that this disconnect can particularly be the case when preservice teacher education programs do not require several years of field experiences as a cornerstone of their program, leading "[m]any [preservice teachers to] feel disillusioned when they encounter the multifaceted nature of teaching, a big part of the shock being taking care of children's emotional needs" (p. 392). Such prolonged stress resulting from their lack of practical classroom experience and difficult mentorship relationships beginning in their teacher education programs might be a reason why 40–50% of teachers leave the field within the first 5 years (Djonko-Moore, 2016; Gold, 1985; Horgan et al., 2018; Ingersoll, 2001). Furthermore, the "stress of inexperience" may continue until they gain the experience necessary to be effective teachers, which takes several years to accomplish (Fantilli & McDougall, 2009). The dearth of scholarship on this issue indicates a need for more empirical work to examine the stress experienced by preservice teachers in general, and more specifically, how these stressors, and potentially others, are experienced by preservice teachers of color.

Preservice Teachers of Color

It is critical to consider the ways in which systemic racism and the privileging of dominant forms of knowledge (i.e., White, cis-male, heterosexual, middle class, etc.) that pervade education systems in the United States and, more specifically, teacher education programs impact preservice teachers of color (Amos, 2010; Carrillo, 2010; Gomez & Rodriguez, 2011; Kohli, 2008; Sheets & Chew, 2002; Weisman & Hansen, 2008). This can even be the case in teacher education programs committed to equity and social justice for pre-K–12 students and the preservice teachers they train (Amos, 2010).

In reference to empirical work by Sleeter (2001), Amos (2010) wrote that "research shows that pre-service students of color 'bring a commitment to multi-cultural teaching, social justice, and providing children of color with an academically challenging curriculum'" (Sleeter, 2001, p. 212, in Amos, 2010, p. 31) in ways that are "higher than that of their White counterparts" (p. 31, in reference to Ladson-Billings, 1991). However, and perhaps because, teacher education programs prepare a predominantly White teaching force (Weisman & Hansen, 2008), much of the curriculum aimed at culturally responsive teaching does not allow for "pre-service students of color [to] . . . extend what they already knew about multicultural pedagogy because the teacher education program was designed for White peers" (Amos, 2010, p. 31).

Attempts at sharing their sociocultural knowledge with their White peers can result in "retaliation and ostracism," leading preservice teachers of color to remain silent in their courses (p. 36). Additionally, it cannot be assumed that being a preservice teacher of color means that they will come into teacher education programs prepared to be culturally responsive teachers even when they feel deeply committed to the work (Weisman & Hansen, 2008). As Whiteness is invasive in curricula at all levels of education (Amos, 2010; Gee, 1996;

Haviland, 2008), many teachers of color may inadvertently take on the practices and discourses of dominant ideologies as preservice teachers as a result of their own educational experiences (Weisman & Hansen, 2008, p. 654).

Complicating "Who" Is a Preservice Teacher of Color

The majority of research on the preparation of preservice teachers of color focuses nearly exclusively "on issues related to recruitment, role models, program models, teacher perception, and mentoring needs of teachers from particular groups of color such as African Americans, Latino Americans, and American Indians" (Sheets & Chew, 2002, p. 128), while often leaving out the experiences and needs of other preservice teachers of color such as Asian Americans (Sheets & Chew, 2002). If one of the goals of contemporary teacher education programs is to recruit and retain diverse teacher candidates, it will be important for researchers to extend scholarship—and for teacher educators to extend their programs—to be more inclusive when it comes to understanding the experiences and needs of preservice teachers of color. Additionally important is examining the ways in which dominant narratives (i.e., White, cis-male, heterosexual, etc.) pervade these programs in order to find ways to authentically support teachers of color in their documented goals of becoming more critically conscious and culturally responsive teachers in the future (Amos, 2010).

In all, it should be clear that preservice teachers are stressed—but what are researchers doing to address that stress? Because a preservice teacher's stress management techniques often mirror how they will manage stress as teachers (Horgan et al., 2018), it is essential to go beyond only identifying the stressors and explore ways to *address* them.

SCHOLARSHIP AIMED AT ADDRESSING PRESERVICE TEACHERS' WELL-BEING

In an extensive review of literature on teacher stress, burnout, and resilience, Beltman et al. (2011) surmised:

> Perhaps reflecting the early stages of research on teacher resilience, a key omission noted in this review was of intervention studies. No work was located where researchers intentionally modified pre-service or early career experiences then systemically examined and compared the impact of different strategies.... Further research is needed to understand the role of pre-service programmes and of teachers themselves in developing resilience. (p. 196)

Though studies have addressed teachers' well-being through mentoring with mixed success (Dingus, 2008; Fantilli & McDougall, 2009) and are beginning to test the utility of mindfulness interventions to reduce the symptoms of stress and burnout felt by teachers (Abenavoli et al., 2013; Beshai et al., 2016; Franco et al., 2010; Hwang et al., 2019a, 2019b; Jennings et al., 2017; Roeser et al., 2013), there is a surprising absence of scholarship aimed at addressing these challenges among preservice teachers—before the effects of potentially overwhelming stress lead to burnout (Wrobel, 2013).

Outside of my own research (Barry, 2021, 2022), my review of the literature led to only one dissertation study in which preservice teachers ($n=67$) participated in a well-being intervention or control group aimed at improving their ability to withstand stress as they eventually transition to becoming teachers (Hirshberg, 2017). The author found:

> that assignment to the well-being training cultivated effective teaching behaviors and mindfulness while reducing implicit race bias, with suggestions of improved self-efficacy and healthy emotionality and reduced implicit negative affect. The magnitude of these effects mostly persisted over a 5–7-month follow-up period. In addition, during the most demanding period of the preservice program, intervention participants were more resilient to developing psychological symptoms and teaching-related burnout. (p. iii)

These findings are promising; however, Hirshberg's participants are reflective of a predominantly White teaching force, with 87% of participants identifying as White (p. 92). Realizing this, he wrote, "this sample may be particularly ill suited to generalizations to more urban, racially diverse areas that tend to have a higher proportion of non-white teachers" (p. 92).

Because researchers have documented that preservice teachers of color experience additional sources of stress during their training (e.g., Amos, 2010), studies aimed at addressing preservice teachers' stress need to pay more attention to how this work can be done in ways that account more thoughtfully for the nuance one's identity brings to their experiences with stress. Furthermore, participants in Hirshberg's (2017) study had to commit to "weekly 1.5-hour classes (for 9 weeks) along with two 4-hour intensive practice days (21.5 hours, total)" (p. 55). Although "4.5 hours occurred during mandated seminar time," these preservice teachers needed to commit to attending well-being practices for 17 hours of their own time and "were asked to practice formally for 10–15 minutes each day and informally many times each day" (p. 55).

As noted by Horgan et al. (2018), "workload . . . time commitments . . . and professional demands such as time management" are major sources of reported stress for preservice teachers (pp. 217–218), which may have made participation in Hirshberg's (2017) study an additional source of stress for the preservice teachers he was attempting to help. Although his findings indicated that these preservice teachers experienced improvements to their well-being (2017) in ways similar to teachers who participated in other mindfulness and well-being interventions aimed at reducing stress and burnout (Jennings et al., 2017; Roeser et al., 2013), intervention studies of this kind must account more thoughtfully for the fact that time itself is a precious commodity among pre- and inservice teachers and that anything detracting from that time—however well-intentioned—may be or become an additional source of stress (Horgan et al., 2018; Kelly & Berthelsen, 1995; Neff et al., 2020).

SELF-COMPASSION: A POTENTIAL WAY FORWARD

Mindfulness and feelings of connection to a community are powerful sources of resilience for teachers of color and White teachers (Dingus, 2008; Jennings et al., 2017). However, there is limited research regarding the utility of bringing these elements together in a single intervention aimed at preventing stress that can lead to burnout and attrition among *all* preservice teachers (Horgan et al., 2018).

What kind of intervention might account for all of these complexities and still be effective? It was my contention in designing the study that guides this book that a simple self-compassion practice, as defined and designed by Neff (2003, 2011), embedded in preservice teachers' training and coursework, may be one way to address these challenges.

What Is Self-Compassion?

As noted earlier, self-compassion involves "three interacting components: self-kindness versus self-judgment, a sense of common humanity versus isolation, and mindfulness versus over-identification when confronting painful self-relevant thoughts and emotions" (Neff & Germer, 2013, p. 28).

In everyday terms:

> Self-compassion involves treating yourself the way you would treat a friend who is having a hard time—even if your friend blew it or is feeling inadequate, or is just facing a tough life challenge. Western culture places great emphasis on being kind to our friends, family, and neighbors who are struggling. Not so when it comes to ourselves. Self-compassion is a practice in which we learn to be a good friend to ourselves when we need it most—to become an inner ally rather than an inner enemy. But typically we don't treat ourselves as well as we treat our friends. (Neff & Germer, 2018, p. 9)

As a former early childhood teacher and now teacher educator, I think about the ways in which self-compassion would have helped me and that I hope it will help the preservice teachers I work with. Perhaps I could have attended better to my own needs and the needs of my students if I hadn't focused solely on the mistakes I was making, which I now understand were inevitable and part of my growth as a teacher. To better understand them, I'll break down these components for you, but remember that they influence each other; and though each has its distinct value, to practice them in *unison* is to practice self-compassion (Neff & Germer, 2018).

Mindfulness. While it "involve[s] paying attention to what's happening in the present moment," mindfulness "also involves a certain quality of attention—accepting what's happening, without being lost in judgments of good or bad" (Neff & Germer, 2018, p. 50). When a person's mindfulness in relation to an experience of suffering is imbued with a sense of self-kindness and the realization that all people experience suffering in varying degrees, their mindfulness practice has become self-compassionate (Neff & Germer, 2013). In this way, self-compassion requires that a person respond to their suffering in the moment with the same kindness they would show a friend who is experiencing the same suffering (Neff & Germer, 2013). In addition to mindfulness, self-compassion involves two additional aspects: self-kindness and common humanity. Together, all three elements of self-compassion are interconnected and influence each other, and cultivating and practicing of each of these elements can "increase" and "enhance one another" (Neff, 2003, p. 89).

Self-Kindness. Neff and Germer (2018) provided readers with a simple definition of self-kindness in *The Mindful Self-Compassion Workbook*:

> When we make a mistake or fail in some way, we are more likely to beat ourselves up than put a supportive arm around our own shoulder. Think of all the generous, caring people you know who constantly tear themselves down (this may even be you). Self-kindness counters this tendency so that we are as caring toward ourselves as we are toward others. Rather than being harshly critical when noticing personal shortcomings, we are supportive and encouraging and aim to protect ourselves from harm. Instead of attacking and berating ourselves for being inadequate, we offer ourselves warmth and unconditional acceptance. Similarly, when external life circumstances are challenging and feel too difficult to bear, we actively soothe and comfort ourselves. (p. 10)

Perhaps in isolation, the definition of self-kindness may make some readers think being kind to themselves in this way is selfish or might "let themselves off the hook" for mistakes they have made. However, self-compassion requires those who practice it to be mindful of the realities of their situations and to consider their connectivity to others as they send kindness to their own suffering. In fact, studies show that people who are more self-compassionate are also more compassionate toward others (Neff & Germer, 2018). When taken together, concerns that self-kindness is selfish or self-indulgent should be dispelled.

Common Humanity. In defining common humanity, Neff and Germer (2018) wrote:

> It's recognizing that all humans are flawed works-in-progress, that everyone fails, makes mistakes, and experiences hardship in life. Self-compassion honors the unavoidable fact that life entails suffering, for everyone, without exception. While this may seem obvious, it's so easy to forget. We fall into the trap of believing that things are "supposed" to go well and that something has gone wrong when they don't. Of course, it's highly likely—in fact inevitable—that we'll make mistakes and experience hardships on a regular basis. This is completely normal and natural. But we don't tend to be rational about these matters. Instead, not only do we suffer, we feel isolated and alone in our suffering. When we remember that pain is part of the shared human experience, however, every moment of suffering is transformed into a moment of connection with others. (pp. 10–11)

In her description of common humanity, Neff (2003) referenced Elkind (1967) when she wrote "the balanced perspective-taking of mindfulness directly counters the egocentrism that causes feelings of isolation and separateness from the rest of humanity, thereby increasing feelings of interconnectedness" (p. 89). This indicates that to be authentically mindful is to be authentically aware of one's reality and thereby must account for the interconnection of all human beings. To do this in a way that is kind—rather than judgmental—is to be self-compassionate.

Misconceptions of Self-Compassion

Self-compassion and how it is measured are not without their critics (e.g., López et al., 2015). As explored earlier, self-compassion is often mistaken for self-centeredness or self-indulgence (Germer & Neff, 2017; Neff, 2011; Neff & Germer, 2018), although, hopefully, at this point in this chapter, these concerns are alleviated. Another misconception of self-compassion is that it is synonymous with self-care (Neff & Germer, 2018), which is explored next.

Self-Compassion Is Different from Self-Care

In a book chapter I wrote on the benefits of practicing self-compassion for teachers of traumatized students (Barry, in Schepers et al., 2023), I reflected on that common misconception:

> Self-compassion, as opposed to self-care, is not something that needs to be delayed or paid for (as self-care practices often are). Self-compassion is a way of relating to and responding to one's challenges and suffering as they arise in the moment with self-kindness, mindfulness, and the understanding that all humans experience challenges and suffering (i.e., common humanity). Self-compassion

does not require that one wait to give themselves the love and kindness they deserve, instead, self-compassion allows people to identify these moments . . . as they arise and respond to them with the same love and care they would to a dear friend (Neff, 2011). Though Corey et al. (2018) wrote that self-care is "an ethical mandate" [for mental health counselors] (p. 3), it is not always accessible in the moments one needs it the most. Self-compassion, however, when cultivated and practiced, is accessible wherever you are, whenever it is needed. (p. 55)

In other words, you don't need a spa day or a room full of aromatherapy candles to practice self-compassion (though if you can do that, go for it!). Self-compassion can be practiced anywhere at any time—even when dealing with the myriad stressors of being a teacher of young children.

Self-Compassion, Teachers, and Preservice Teachers

Self-compassion has reduced stress (Shapiro et al., 2005), increased job satisfaction (Barnard & Curry, 2012), and reduced the negative effects of empathy fatigue among professional caregivers (Eriksson et al., 2018; Neff & Germer, 2018; Sinclair et al., 2017). As such, practicing self-compassion may be one way that preservice teachers can manage their stress and stay in their classrooms healthfully and sustainably with the skills needed to be the teacher their students deserve and to care for themselves in ways *they* deserve (Barry, 2021, 2022, 2023). Furthermore, developing these self-compassionate habits sooner rather than later (i.e., while enrolled in teacher education programs) may be a way to ease or even prevent pre- and inservice teachers' experiences with empathy fatigue, burnout, and stress in the present and future (Gold, 1985; Horgan et al., 2018) that lead to such startling attrition rates among novice teachers (Barry, 2023; Djonko-Moore, 2016; Fantilli & McDougall, 2009; Ingersoll, 2001). To do this could address many concerns raised by scholars regarding reducing stress and burnout among teachers in general and teachers of color specifically (Ingersoll & Connor, 2009; Ryan et al., 2017). As noted earlier in this chapter, how preservice teachers begin to deal with stress has implications for how they will deal with it in the future (Gold, 1985; Horgan et al., 2018), which makes their teacher education program a particularly critical moment in their career trajectory to address these challenges.

SCHOLARLY ATTEMPTS AT REDUCING STRESS AMONG PRESERVICE EARLY CHILDHOOD TEACHERS

Mindfulness-based interventions have been successful at mitigating stress and burnout among educators (e.g., Jennings et al., 2017), but there have been very few of these studies, and there are still many unknowns regarding how these interventions are experienced by teachers of color and White teachers working in urban contexts (Jennings et al., 2017). These interventions are also lengthy and have required teachers to volunteer their out-of-school time to participate (Jennings et al., 2017; Roeser et al., 2013). As a lack of time is a source of stress among teachers (Kelly & Berthelsen, 1995) and preservice teachers (Horgan et al., 2018), interventions aimed at alleviating stress should not become an additional source of stress because of the time required to participate (Neff et al., 2020). Furthermore, given the unique experiences of stress a teacher will feel in relation to their work is highly contextualized and based on who they are and how they identify in a myriad of ways (e.g., gender identity, sexuality, race, ethnicity, language, religion, etc.), it is hard for a variety of predetermined interventions to be blanketly applicable to all participants. While experience with a variety of practices aimed at reducing stress among teachers and preservice teachers may be helpful, the many weeks these intervention studies take will mean it will take even longer for those who practice them to determine which works best for them.

Additionally, it is important to note that there is limited knowledge regarding the impact of interventions from the Mindful Self-Compassion Program (MSC) (Neff & Germer, 2018) among teachers and preservice teachers in general or teachers and preservice teachers of color specifically (Barry, 2021, 2022). This is a missed opportunity, particularly because of the isolation experienced by pre- and inservice teachers in general (Chang, 2009) and pre- and inservice teachers of color specifically (Amos, 2010; Dingus, 2008). Therefore, *the deliberate inclusion of practices geared toward the experience of common humanity—an essential element of self-compassion—could be extraordinarily beneficial for mitigating the stress and burnout felt as a result of that isolation.*

Further, to be mindful of one's suffering does not necessarily mean that one will be kind to themselves in that moment of suffering. As evidenced by studies of professional caregivers with high self-compassion scores, self-kindness is essential when it comes to dealing with the constant compassion and empathy extended to those in their care (Amrani, 2010; Benzo et al., 2017; Eriksson et al., 2018; Finlay-Jones et al., 2015; Knier et al., 2020; Montero-Marin et al., 2016; Neff et al., 2020; Sinclair et al., 2017; Stebnicki, 2015; Yela et al., 2019) and to ensure they don't succumb to the harmful effects of empathy fatigue (Stebnicki, 2015) and burnout (Maslach & Leiter, 2016).

Although the challenges and omissions explored here are many, the gaps reveal opportunities. As such, embedding self-compassion practice in preservice teachers' teacher education programs holds promise for addressing their experiences with stress, burnout, and possible attrition in the future. My dissertation research, on which this book is based, attempted to fill this gap in a way that would address all three components of self-compassion without triggering additional stressors for the preservice teachers who so generously agreed to be part of my study (Barry, 2021). To do this, I knew it would be important to give preservice teachers time *within* classes and fieldwork to practice self-compassion. I believed—and still believe—that doing so could alleviate the stress other interventions may have caused by requiring teachers' limited free time (e.g., Hirshberg, 2017). Second, I felt it was essential to ensure that these practices were personally relevant to each preservice teacher's experience of contextualized stress, that they encouraged feelings of connection, and that they were imbued with self-kindness. These factors begged the question: What self-compassion practice or practices would be most effective for preservice teachers?

A Self-Compassion Practice For Preservice Teachers

In Neff's (2011) book *Self-Compassion,* she shared a variety of strategies and practices that have been empirically validated to increase self-compassion (Neff & Germer, 2018). Due to the unique stress experienced by preservice teachers, I found one of Neff's self-compassion exercises particularly appropriate: Exploring Self-Compassion Through Letter Writing (Neff, 2011, pp. 16–17). It is a writing exercise that I believe may serve as an effective entry point for people just beginning their self-compassion practice because the practice requires them to actually produce something (i.e., a written letter) rather than meditate. The creation of a piece (or pieces) of writing that preservice teachers can revisit may also serve as a concrete record of their journey toward becoming more self-compassionate. Furthermore, the ability to see their documented growth on this journey may be inspiring when dealing with particularly difficult circumstances at school and may motivate them to continue practicing self-compassion—perhaps even stay in the teaching profession after completing their teacher education program (Barry, 2021, 2022, 2023).

Most compelling, it turns out my hunch was correct among the preservice teachers in my study; the self-compassionate writing practice I highlight next was effective for the preservice teachers in my dissertation research. In fact, they experienced a significant increase in their self-compassion scores over their three semesters of field experiences and coursework in their teacher education program with a large Cohen's D effect size of .77 (Barry, 2021, 2022, 2023). (See Appendix B for participant demographic information and statistical tests.)

The letter-writing activity I engaged the preservice teachers with in my dissertation study came from Neff's (2011) self-compassion exercise titled Exploring Self-Compassion Through Letter Writing. I asked them to consider "an issue that tends to make [them] feel inadequate or bad about [themselves]" and to "feel [their] emotions [connected to this issue] exactly as they are—no more, no less" (p. 16). Using Neff's (2011) prompt, these preservice teachers were then directed to

> think about an imaginary friend who is unconditionally loving, accepting, kind, and compassionate. Imagine that this friend can see all your strengths and all your weaknesses, including the aspect of yourself you have just been thinking about. . . . This friend recognizes the limits of human nature and is kind and forgiving towards you. (p. 16)

They were then prompted to "[w]rite a letter to [themselves] from the perspective of this imaginary friend" (p. 17) using the following questions written by Neff to guide their letter:

> What would this friend say to you about your "flaw" from the perspective of unlimited compassion? How would this friend convey the deep compassion he/she feels for you, especially for the discomfort you feel when you judge yourself so harshly? What would this friend write in order to remind you that you are only human, that all people have both strengths and weaknesses? And if you think this friend would suggest possible changes you should make, how would these suggestions embody feelings of unconditional understanding and compassion? As you write to yourself from the perspective of this imaginary friend, try to infuse your letter with a strong sense of the person's acceptance, kindness, caring, and desire for your health and happiness. (p. 17)

This practice may be particularly useful because the preservice teachers writing the letters pick the sources of stress, failure, or inadequacy that are most personally relevant to write about.

Although some self-compassionate writing interventions have been explored in the literature (not with preservice teachers), these studies have had mixed results when it has come to their effectiveness (Dreisoerner et al., 2020; Wong & Mak, 2016). In one such study, the researchers did not use the specific prompt written by Neff (2011), which resulted in "awkward" responses from participants that "had no explicit mindfulness component" and lacked some "clarity" (Dreisoerner et al., 2020, p. 20). Had the researchers utilized Neff's Exploring Self-Compassion Through Letter Writing (2011), the writing samples collected from participants could have had clearer connections to the particular challenge the participant wrote about and all three components of self-compassion (Dreisoerner et al., 2020).

What I found most compelling about Neff's prompt (2011) was that the preservice teacher writing the letter could choose the words, phrases, and overall tone of the real or imagined dear friend rather than being directed how to do so. Because they chose the words and phrases they needed to hear, preservice teachers gave themselves the feedback *they* would like to receive. Having this much freedom in how to respond with compassion to their suffering may therefore be particularly useful to early childhood teachers at any career stage. If preservice teachers are given the time to write these letters to themselves over the course of their teacher education, they may also be given the skills needed to protect themselves against burnout and attrition in the future (Barry, 2023). Furthermore, *Neff's (2011) exercise has been shown to be a useful intervention for preservice teachers in general and preservice teachers of color specifically because it invites them to speak directly to their individual and unique experiences with stress and perceived failure in ways that are not only personally relevant, mindful, and kind but also promotive of feelings of connectedness to others* (Barry, 2021, 2022, 2023). Practices like these can be particularly powerful at reducing the feelings of isolation that pre- and inservice teachers in general and pre- and inservice teachers of color in particular frequently report as sources of attrition (e.g., Milner & Hoy, 2003).

CHAPTER 2

My Mixed-Methods Case Study
The Impact of Self-Compassion Practice on Preservice Teachers

To investigate the impact of practicing self-compassion among preservice teachers as they progressed through a teacher education program, I implemented a mixed-methods case study (Creswell & Plano Clark, 2017). Specifically, I examined how a cohort of preservice teachers ($n = 16$) enrolled in a large, urban university teacher education program participated in an empirically validated self-compassion practice (Neff & Germer, 2013) over the course of their three required semesters of field placements and coursework in urban elementary schools. I wanted to understand what the unique sources of their stress as preservice early childhood teachers were, how they responded to those stressors with self-compassion, and if the practice made a difference in how they experienced stressors and challenges.

Much of the research on teacher attrition (e.g., Ingersoll, 2001) and teachers' work-related stress (e.g., Fantilli & McDougall, 2009) relies heavily on quantitative data sources. Though this work has illuminated several aspects of teachers' unique experiences of stress, burnout, and attrition, the studies are not able to illuminate the nuance and deeply personal factors that influence a teacher to check off "general job dissatisfaction" (Ingersoll, 2001) on a survey when asked about their stress, burnout, and attrition. For this reason, it is important for research that explores these phenomena to also include qualitative data sources (e.g., interviews) that attend to this nuance. Such qualitative data allows researchers to present "rich, thick description . . . as a strategy to [provide] . . . a detailed description of the findings with adequate evidence presented in the form of quotes from participant interviews, field notes, and documents" (Merriam & Tisdell, 2016, p. 257) in ways that quantitative data alone cannot. Further, because of the myriad of factors that influence pre- and inservice teachers' experiences with stress (e.g., school governance policies, levels of support, etc.), using case study as a research methodology gives researchers the opportunity to generate findings with "an in-depth description and analysis of a bounded system" (p. 37). This means that the data collected and analyzed are specific to that particular case, and "the researcher has an obligation to provide enough detailed description of the study's context to enable readers to compare the 'fit' with their situations" (p. 256) through the rich description and triangulation (p. 259) of multiple data sources—both quantitative and qualitative (Creswell & Plano Clark, 2017). Therefore, this study that guided this book—an investigation of how a particular self-compassion practice mitigated stress with a diverse group of preservice teachers over the course of their training—lent itself to mixed-methods case study design. Furthermore, this work complements, adds depth, and offers potential future directions to the extant research on pre- and inservice teachers' experiences of stress, burnout, and attrition.

RECRUITING PARTICIPANTS AND DATA COLLECTION

I began recruiting in the fall of 2018 after a cohort coordinator expressed to me a deep interest in making self-compassion practice a part of her monthly seminars for her cohort of preservice teachers' three semesters of field placements and coursework. As a former elementary school principal, she was keenly aware of the stress teachers experience and was committed to helping this group of preservice teachers protect themselves from the potentially damaging effects of that stress. This cohort coordinator was also a participant in this study, as was another cohort coordinator and several field supervisors ($n = 5$) who observed and evaluated these and other preservice teachers who were enrolled in the program. Their inclusion was my attempt to present findings triangulated from data sources that go beyond self-reports, which are often cited as limitations in self-compassion research (e.g., Finlay-Jones et al., 2015) and research with preservice teachers (Horgan et al., 2018).

I gave a 10-minute PowerPoint presentation early in their first semester (fall 2018) about my study and what I would be asking of these preservice teachers as participants. I answered their questions and then disseminated and collected their consent forms and their first-semester self-compassion scales. I appended Neff's Self-Compassion Scale: Short Form (Raes et al., 2011) (see Appendix A) to my consent forms so that each preservice teacher who wished to participate could complete it within their first semester so that I could statistically analyze how their self-reported self-compassion levels changed over time.

I was pleased to see that many of the preservice teachers chose to participate ($n = 16$) and expressed that they were invested in being involved for the remainder of my data collection, which I concluded in June 2020 after they graduated and were completing their first year of teaching.

Participant Identities

It should be noted that over half of the preservice teachers in this study identified as women of color (see Appendix B for participant demographics). Although "[s]elf-compassion appears to foster well-being among all people, regardless of gender, age, or culture" (Yarnell et al., 2015, p. 3), the majority of people who access self-compassion courses tend to be middle-aged White women (p. 3). That said, researchers have begun to evaluate how women of color experience participation in self-compassion interventions (e.g., Finlay-Jones et al., 2017; Wong & Mak, 2016). This study is therefore timely and novel in that it extends studies of self-compassion to include participants who are diverse in terms of their sociocultural identity and the benefits they experienced from practicing self-compassion.

Because it was not up to me—nor do I feel it was appropriate for me—to decide for the participants what aspects of their identity were most relevant to how they identified themselves, I instead asked each participant for an identity statement in which they described what they felt were the most important aspects of their identity (e.g., race, gender, religion, relationships with family and friends, hobbies, etc.). Specific stressors connected to their racial identities only came up three times in our interviews and did not come up in any other data sources.

My Positionality in Relation to This Work

As a gay, tall, White, loud-laughing, cis-male professor and former pre-K and kindergarten teacher, I try to be aware of how my positionality, privilege, and experience impact my interactions with others. I deliberately dress down to avoid being mistaken for an administrator when field supervising in public elementary schools and to appear more approachable as a professor. My experience as a kindergarten teacher taught me a lot about how my tone, facial expressions, and the way I position and move my body can—and do—influence the interactions I have with others, and I have worked hard to develop a demeanor that makes others feel comfortable.

Although I cannot always know how my efforts are received by others, I was moved by the fact that so many of the preservice teachers from the cohort I recruited from sought out the opportunity to be involved in my study. As a result of my awareness of my positionality and the sincere care I had for them, I was deeply committed to writing about them in ways that were non-essentializing. I believe conducting this research as a case study assisted me in this endeavor. Utilizing case study methods can help researchers avoid essentializing because generalizing to larger populations is not a goal of case study research; rather, readers determine if the findings of the study are rigorous, credible, and relevant to their own situations (Merriam & Tisdell, 2016, p. 256).

Data Sources and Collection—Quantitative Data

The preservice teachers in my study completed Neff's Self-Compassion Scale: Short Form (Raes et al., 2011) (see Appendix A) once every semester while enrolled in their teacher education program ($n = 3$). Once completed, statistical tests were administered to determine if any significant changes in their self-compassion ratings had occurred. Several rationales led to the methodological choice to use the short form to measure participants' self-compassion. As mentioned earlier, time is a limited resource among preservice teachers, and as Neff (2011) wrote:

> "the shortened, 12-item [self-compassion scale] can be effectively and efficiently used as an economical alternative to the full SCS. The SCS–SF may be of particular use in time and cost-intensive survey and therapy outcome research, often containing loaded test batteries" (p. 254). Furthermore, the shortened scale "demonstrated adequate internal consistency (Cronbach's alpha ≥ 0.86 in all samples) and a near-perfect correlation with the long form SCS ($r \geq 0.97$ all samples)." (p. 250)

Neff (2011) recommended using the long form if a researcher sought to analyze the subscales (mindfulness, self-kindness, and common humanity). Given that my aim was to measure their overall self-compassion and not wanting to ask any more of them than absolutely necessary, I decided to use the short form. Other researchers have used the short form with great success (Benzo et al., 2017; Finlay-Jones et al., 2015).

Data Sources and Collection—Qualitative Data

Through the collection of a variety of artifacts—which included the self-compassionate letters written by the preservice teachers; their three sets of fieldwork journals (which were required in their teacher education program); and two rounds of semi-structured interviews and member checks with the preservice teachers, their field supervisors, and cohort coordinators (who evaluate their progress in the teacher education program)—I began to uncover the unique challenges that caused these preservice teachers' stress and how participation in the self-compassionate letter-writing intervention appeared to ease that stress.

For approximately 10 to 15 minutes during their seminars, each participant wrote a self-compassionate letter to themselves from the perspective of "an imaginary friend who is unconditionally loving, accepting, kind, and compassionate" by responding to Neff's (2011) "exploring self-compassion through letter writing" prompt (p. 16) to address a recent feeling of stress, failure, or inadequacy in their field placements or coursework. Some handwrote their letters, while others typed their letters and submitted them electronically either by email or Google form.

Those who handwrote their letter photographed it to keep for themselves to read over whenever they wished and turned in the original letter to me for coding and analysis. Those who typed their letter had electronic access to it since it was submitted by email or Google form (both of which they had access to after completion). Willing participants were interviewed at the midpoint of the teacher education program (spring 2019) and in their first year of teaching (spring 2020).

I found that what these preservice teachers shared with me in their fieldwork journals, self-compassionate letters, and interviews was deeply personal and generous. As a result of the deeply personal nature of this study, this work would likely yield different findings if done with different preservice teachers or if a different researcher had attempted to do the work with this group. However, as Merriam and Tisdell wrote (2016), "Replication of a qualitative study will not yield the same results, but this does not discredit the results of any particular study. . . . The more important question . . . is whether the results are consistent with the data collected" (p. 251). To address this, I implemented several strategies qualitative researchers utilize to ensure my findings were consistent and credible (p. 244). For example, I triangulated multiple data sources (Merriam & Tisdell, 2016) and conducted the research as a mixed-method case study. By converging the quantitative and multiple qualitative data sources, I was able to provide more credible findings (Creswell & Plano Clark, 2017; Merriam & Tisdell, 2016).

Data Analysis—Quantitative Data

Quantitative analysis of Neff's Self-Compassion Scale: Short Form (Raes et al., 2011) was done in SPSS using paired sample t-tests. These statistical tests allow researchers to examine how a particular group changes over time on a particular measure quantitatively, identifies when significant changes occur between time periods, and calculates the effect sizes (Cohen's d) of those significant changes and if the degree of the significance is small, medium, or large. The group mean for semester 1 was compared using t-tests to the group mean of semester 2, semester 2 to semester 3, and semester 1 to semester 3 (see Appendix B for participant demographic information and statistical results).

Data Analysis—Qualitative Data

The interviews with the preservice teachers, the field supervisors, and cohort coordinators were audio-recorded, transcribed, masked, and coded using a set of external codes (Graue & Walsh, 1998) based on the theoretical orientations that guided this study (i.e., self-compassion practice could mitigate the effects of stress, empathy fatigue, and burnout with preservice teachers). Through the constant-comparative method (Merriam & Tisdell, 2016, p. 208) some internal codes were developed (Graue & Walsh, 1998). For example, from constantly comparing and triangulating my data, codes such as "mistakes are learning opportunities" and "positive relationships with students" were generated. The self-compassionate letters these preservice teachers wrote were analyzed to determine what specific stressors were most often written about and how they chose to address those stressors with self-compassion. Qualitative analysis was done in NVIVO 12.

Trustworthiness

These multiple sources of data and methods of data collection enabled me to present credible findings by way of triangulation and member-checking (Merriam & Tisdell, 2016, p. 244). For example, by converging quantitative data (i.e., the self-compassion scores) with qualitative data (i.e., interview data), I was able to build and report more credible findings (Creswell & Plano Clark, 2018; Merriam & Tisdell, 2016). In order to understand the particular challenges these preservice teachers experienced over time in the teacher education program, the data sources that most directly addressed their challenges were their three semesters of fieldwork journals and the interviews with the preservice teachers, the cohort coordinators, and the field supervisors. These data sources were then converged in order to find out what particular challenges and stressors the preservice teachers experienced.

To understand how these preservice teachers were impacted by the self-compassion practice in their teacher education program, my quantitative data (i.e., the self-compassion scores) and qualitative data (preservice teachers' interviews regarding their experiences with practicing self-compassion and their perceptions of the benefits) were converged to bring a deeper understanding to how they felt about practicing self-compassion and how practicing self-compassion appeared to impact their self-compassion scores over time. By interviewing participants multiple times over the course of the study, I was able to member-check (Merriam & Tisdell, 2016, p. 246) and ask follow-up and clarifying questions in the second interview I conducted with them, which was another credibility measure I employed.

As the majority of data sources for this study were self-reported (e.g., self-compassion scores, interviews, etc.), an additional triangulation "strategy for increasing the credibility . . . of [this] research" (Merriam & Tisdell, 2016, p. 245) was the inclusion of the perspectives of the cohort coordinators ($n=2$) and field supervisors ($n=5$) who mentored and evaluated the preservice teachers. The data from these semi-structured interviews allowed me to gain additional insight into the challenges they experienced and how practicing self-compassion appeared to impact them from a "qualified" observer's perspective. As Patton (2015) wrote, including these additional perspectives and data sources "increases credibility and quality by countering the concern . . . that a study's findings are simply an artifact of a single method, . . . source, or a single investigator's blinders" (p. 674).

By conducting this research using a mixed-methods case study methodology, I was able to shine a spotlight (Thomas, 2016) on a particular group of preservice teachers and to collect, analyze, and converge multiple data sources—both qualitative and quantitative—to understand what the specific stressors these preservice teachers experienced were and how self-compassion practice helped them in addressing those stressors (Creswell & Plano Clark, 2018). Further, the use of this methodology presented the opportunity for me to give readers enough "rich, thick description" (Merriam & Tisdell, 2016, p. 256) to decide whether or not my findings can generalize to their circumstances.

Finally, because this is a mixed-methods case study, the findings assist me in speaking on the issues of teacher stress and burnout to multiple audiences who situate themselves as quantitative, qualitative, and mixed-methodologists. Bringing these issues to the attention of researchers who utilize particular methodologies in their work holds possibilities for the future of scholarship aimed at addressing teachers' unique experiences of stress, burnout, and attrition with self-compassion.

FINDINGS: SELF-COMPASSION PRACTICE MATTERED TO THESE PRESERVICE TEACHERS

To find out if participation in this self-compassionate letter-writing practice yielded benefits for these preservice teachers, I held two rounds of semi-structured interviews with them to learn how they felt about participating in the exercises across their enrollment in this teacher education program. They were interviewed at the halfway point (mid-semester 2) and after graduation in order to learn how they felt about writing the letters during the study and then again, retrospectively. This was also a way to address the credibility of this research through member-checking (Merriam & Tisdell, 2016). Additionally, the preservice teachers filled out Neff's Self-Compassion Scale: Short Form (Raes et al., 2011) once each semester throughout their enrollment in this teacher education program.

To converge these data sources that illuminate how these preservice teachers' self-compassion ratings changed over time and their reflections on participating in the letter-writing offered insight into the utility of this exercise. As higher levels of self-compassion are associated with lower instances of job-related stress and burnout among professional caregivers, my belief was that the same would be true for these preservice teachers (Barnard & Curry, 2012; Delaney, 2018; Duarte et al., 2016; Eriksson et al., 2018; Finlay-Jones et al., 2015; Knier et al., 2020; Neff et al., 2020; Stebnicki, 2015; Yela et al., 2019).

I also included data from interviews I held with these preservice teachers' field supervisors ($n=5$) and cohort coordinators ($n=2$) to demonstrate their perceptions of the utility of these preservice teachers participating in the self-compassionate letter writing exercise to address their experiences with challenges, stressors, and feelings of inadequacy throughout their time in the teacher education program. By triangulating and converging these data sources (Creswell & Plano Clark, 2017; Merriam & Tisdell, 2016), I found that self-compassion did in fact matter to these preservice teachers and might help them better address stress and withstand burnout as future teachers (Barry, 2023).

Preservice Teachers' Early Impressions of Self-Compassionate Letter Writing

In the following section, I present data from semi-structured interviews with these preservice teachers at the midpoint of their enrollment in this teacher education program. All interviewed preservice teachers ($n=10$) chose their own pseudonyms (as did the interviewed cohort coordinators and field supervisors). My analysis and coding process resulted in four themes (Merriam & Tisdell, 2016) that illuminate the ways in which these preservice teachers reflected on their participation in the self-compassionate letter-writing exercise:

1. Self-Compassion Works to Address Future Burnout and Current Stress
2. Self-Compassionate Letter Writing Gets Easier Over Time
3. Being Self-Compassionate May Impact Students
4. Participants Have Critiques of Self-Compassionate Letter Writing

Self-Compassion Works to Address Future Burnout and Current Stress. All preservice teachers interviewed at the midpoint of the teacher education program ($n=10$) indicated that they felt practicing self-compassion had helped them manage their stress and would continue to help them when they become teachers. For example, Anna said:

> I think [self-compassion] can definitely help fight against the burnout feeling. . . . [B]eing aware of what's going on, objectively just kinda helps you keep going. Because if you're always wrapped up in the emotions, you're dealing with parents, you may be having a challenging time with students, or your administration, you're always just feeling so much stress versus taking a few minutes out of the day to just take a step back from that, intentionally.

Elaine's statement expanded on Anna's sentiments:

> I think [self-compassion] is probably the most important thing because I think a lot of teachers get burnt out because they don't take care of themselves and

they forget that they are also human and that they need that. They need positive reassurance from themselves. . . . I mean if you don't take care of yourself, how are you gonna take care of other people, you know?

In a heartfelt description, Quinn said:

> I think it's [self-compassion] 100% necessary. . . . I just think teaching in particular is one [job] that people get so burnt out on so fast because it takes so much emotional energy. And if you can't learn how to handle that in a way that's mostly positive for yourself, you're going to go through a lot of really negative consequences that are probably going to make it seem like teaching's just not worth it.

Combined, not only did the preservice teachers appear to find the practice of self-compassion necessary, they also seemed to believe that by practicing self-compassion they could protect themselves from burning out when they became teachers in the future. As researchers have found, a teacher's stress can lead to burnout and burnout can lead to teacher attrition (Abenavoli et al., 2013; Ryan et al., 2017; Westervelt, 2016; Wrobel, 2013). Furthermore, researchers have found that a teacher's relationship with stress—whether it be positive or maladaptive—begins in their preservice teacher education (Horgan et al., 2018, pp. 217–218). It seems that these preservice teachers believed that practicing self-compassion was one way in which they managed their stress in the present (i.e., in their teacher education program) that might also protect them from burnout in the future.

Although these statements reflect these preservice teachers' impressions of burnout specifically, they also discussed how the self-compassionate letter-writing practice was helpful at addressing their stress in the moment. For example, Alycia said:

> I think [self-compassionate letter writing] does help. Like, I'm not jumping to the bad things and it makes me take a step back and just reassess. I feel like before I would panic and not know exactly how I would react.

Leslie expressed a similar benefit to Alycia when it came to "not jumping to the bad things" that she attributed to self-compassion:

> I think it's really important cause I mean, it's really stressful, like, the TEP [teacher education program] is a lot, you know? And we're also going through the TEP and our actual lives, so it's just a lot of stress overall. And I think it's important to remind ourselves to have self-compassion. I think it's, like, really just a reminder for us to just don't be so hard on ourselves. I know I talked to a lot of people in the TEP and they said that we're just all stressed—or we were. And so it's just, like, really cool to see that, to remember that we're human and that

we're going to make mistakes sometimes so we shouldn't, you know, just hate ourselves for that, you know, if we mess up.

Finally, Amy described what she felt what it was specifically about the self-compassionate letter-writing practice that she believed made it such a powerful exercise for her in addressing her stress in the teacher education program. She said:

> The believing in you[rself] part, which is—I think is, I mean it's the message I'm getting from my family all the time and they're trying to support me through this and, hearing it I guess for myself about a specific event it's so much more helpful. With my family, they can say, "oh, I know you're struggling with this, you have a lot of work and I know you can do it." It's a general encompassing statement. They don't really know what I'm struggling with even though they're trying to support me through it. But because I know what my struggle is, and I am doing my best to be kind to myself, I am able to believe it more. After writing those [self-compassionate letters] I went into the classroom so much more confident. Like, "you know what? I'm not gonna do that today, I'm gonna figure out how NOT to do that today! I'm gonna do better."

Here, Amy expressed what is perhaps most powerful about the self-compassionate letter-writing exercise. Though each person experiences suffering and challenges, "[t]he triggers are different, the circumstances are different, [and] the degree of pain is different" (Neff, 2011, p. 62), which means what each person needs when addressing their suffering will be nuanced based on who they are and what the circumstance is that has caused them pain. Although Amy seemed to appreciate her family's support, she also acknowledged that she is the only person who "know[s] what [her] struggle is" and for that reason, may be the only person who knows what kind of support she needed to address that "struggle." For Amy, being able to speak to her struggle with a complete understanding and giving herself the compassion she needed to address it seemed to be what she perceived as one of the benefits of participating in the exercise.

Self-Compassionate Letter Writing Gets Easier Over Time. Many of these preservice teachers also noted that the letter-writing exercise became easier with time and practice. For example, Selena said:

> Yeah, I feel like with other people it's always easy . . . but with myself, it was always like, "well, I'm the worst person ever. Why did I even do that?" But it was just affecting my overall attitude towards myself. It was like, it was like I was putting myself last, I guess. So, like with the [self-compassionate letter writing], it just keeps me accountable. Like, "Hey, you know, you did have a bad day, but whatever, like it's fine. It's okay. You don't have to beat yourself up for the rest of the week."

Selena found supporting other people easier than supporting herself. As Neff and Germer (2018) wrote, "Western culture places great emphasis on being kind to our friends, family, and neighbors who are struggling. Not so when it comes to ourselves" (p. 9), which may be connected to Selena's challenges in being self-compassionate. For her, it seemed that writing these letters kept her "accountable" for being self-compassionate rather than "beat[ing her] self up for the rest of the week."

Quinn expanded on Selena's statement about why practicing self-compassion was harder for her at first but got easier:

> I think at first it's a lot harder than it is later on. Because a lot of us just aren't taught to think like that and I think it might be like a cultural thing with American culture. We really value individualism and I think that in a lot of ways we put really harsh expectations on ourselves that are really unrealistic. And I think writing those self-compassionate letters at first felt very difficult and kind of silly, I guess. Like it feels weird. I definitely doubted it like the first couple times I came into contact with it 'cause I've had problems all my life. This one little trick isn't really going to solve them, you know? But I think it really does because I think I could just start to adjust the schemas that you have in your brain to when something goes wrong or you experience a negative feeling, instead of going straight towards blaming yourself or making the situation worse, you've spent some time like reflecting on how to be kinder to yourself and analyze the situation in a more rational way. And I think that makes it a lot easier too, eventually. So definitely at first like I, as I started being able to be self-compassionate, it would be like, in reflection later on, you know? Because it's hard in the moment if that's not what you're used to; it's really hard to start thinking like that. But I would say more and more I stopped having to reframe things as much, and that's just the way I thought.

Here, Quinn echoed Selena's statement about how difficult it was to relate to her challenges in her field placement with self-compassion because it was not how she was used to relating to herself. Though at first Quinn doubted that this practice would be helpful because she had "problems all [her] life," she expressed that with time and practice, relating to herself with self-compassion became "just the way [she] thought."

Bob's experience with the self-compassionate letter writing also seemed to become easier with time. In her midpoint interview, she said:

> Okay—I love it. At first, I was a little bit like, "this is weird . . . 'dear me'"? You know? That was interesting. At first it felt a little bit forced. Like I was trying to just say nice things to myself. But then after a while I just felt happier 'cause I was like "we're going to say nice things to ourselves, this is so exciting!" So that really helped. And I think it also helped my inner voice kind of just say nicer things. Like I get tempted so many times a day to be like, "oh this day stinks.

I'm not going to have a great day. These kids aren't listening to me" and just telling myself "it's okay just take it slowly. You're doing great." Things like that. I feel like that really helped.

For these preservice teachers, what began as a challenging or awkward exercise in developing self-compassion through letter writing became a way in which they began relating to the challenges they experienced in the moment as they arose. In addition to becoming "easier" with practice, they also described feeling that this self-compassionate letter-writing exercise also began to influence how they went about their work with their students; that this practice not only benefited them as future teachers but might benefit their students as well.

Being Self-Compassionate May Impact Students. During the midpoint interviews, some of these preservice teachers expressed that their self-compassion practice might benefit their current and future students by encouraging students to also be self-compassionate when relating to their own challenges. Bob explained how she was currently trying to do this with students:

> I feel like people are very hard on themselves and I've seen this with kids, which is so sad. I've heard so many kids say I'm stupid or I can't do this. And so my mission was to make them change their minds about themselves. I was like, "no, we need to love ourselves." And so I just constantly remind kids, "we're not going to say that we can't do this" and support each other too. If someone's struggling, don't just watch them, tell them "you can do this, I believe in you."

It seemed important to Bob to model self-compassionate language aloud to her students when they would say they were "stupid" or could not accomplish a task in class as well as to encourage connection among students (i.e., common humanity) when they witnessed a classmate struggling. In this way, Bob encouraged her students to both "change their minds about themselves" and support each other.

Anna believed that self-compassion practice would benefit her students in ways similar to Bob:

> I can definitely see too incorporating it with students. You know, whenever students are really frustrated, maybe when they're not getting a concept and it's bothering them. 'Cause I'm seeing that in my placement now. The kids get test anxiety. Or they're just so upset with themselves that they're not "getting it" when all their other peers are able to. If they write the [self-compassionate] letter to themselves, it introduces [self-compassion] at an early age. I feel like if it's introduced as early as then, you know, what could happen later is pretty great. Like, how would you go through problems and process problems later in life if you already had that in your mental backpack?

What Anna described here is precisely why I chose this particular self-compassion exercise to implement with her and the other preservice teachers in this study; that to start these practices early, before becoming teachers, held potential to equip them with the skills necessary to avoid feeling debilitated by stress or feelings of inadequacy, as self-compassion practice has been shown to do among professional caregivers (Barnard & Curry, 2012; Delaney, 2018; Duarte et al., 2016; Eriksson et al., 2018; Finlay-Jones et al., 2015; Knier et al., 2020; Neff et al., 2020; Stebnicki, 2015; Yela et al., 2019). Here, Anna extrapolated on this by saying that supporting her elementary-aged students in developing self-compassion skills as children would equip them to manage stressors and challenges later in life in ways that were self-compassionate rather than self-critical (Neff, 2003; Neff, 2011; Neff & Germer, 2018).

Quinn seemed to share in Bob and Anna's beliefs about how modeling self-compassion to students could also benefit students:

> I think being able to be self-compassionate in front of your students is just such a great way to teach them how to become later on. I feel like I'm learning a lot of things about SEL [social-emotional learning] and myself just from learning about how to teach kids. These are things I never learned and I definitely should've learned. You know? It would've saved me like a lot of negative feelings and stuff. I think that when we can do that and model it to kids, I think that we're just setting them up [for] so much more of the joy of life, like, just being able to get through adversity in a less painful way. And just teaching them to take on challenges even if they're kind of scary or we might mess up. I think just showing kids that you're human too, and like, here's some great ways to deal with being human. I think that that's just a really, really good thing for them. You know?

So many of the challenges these preservice teachers experienced throughout their teacher education program were related to not feeling like a teacher and not being seen as a teacher by others. Here, however, Quinn expressed that she believes giving her students opportunities to see her as a "human" who "mess[es] up" would actually support students in "get[ting] through adversity in a less painful way." It seemed that Quinn believed that demonstrating her capacity to find learning opportunities within her mistakes to her students could encourage them to do the same (e.g., Johnston, 2003).

Alycia also believed that her self-compassion practice might influence her students, but that the influence would have more to do with the climate in her cooperating teacher's classroom. She said:

> I think [self-compassion is] important because you're basically assessing yourself and how you're doing. I think you do need to pay attention to it—where you're at and how you're doing—because it will reflect on your teaching and the

students will pick up on it. I feel like if you're not assessing how you're doing you'll just be more anxious, and it'll show; it'll reflect on the students and how they feel in the class.

For Alycia, "assessing how [she was]" in the moment (i.e., being mindful) helped her appear less "anxious" in front of her students. Furthermore, it seemed that she felt it would be better to appear less "anxious" because her anxiety might impact "how [her students] feel in [her] class."

Although all of these preservice teachers expressed that there were a variety of benefits from writing their self-compassionate letters, two of them, Elaine and Maria, also shared critiques about the practice.

Participants Have Critiques of Self-Compassionate Letter Writing. While Elaine and Maria both said they benefited in many ways from participating in the self-compassionate letter-writing exercise when we spoke at the midpoint of the teacher education program, each of them had a critique that feels important to share. For example, Elaine found the exercise to be repetitive:

> Before we started doing this self-compassion thing, I never really noticed how negatively I talked to myself about certain things. Like I would never say like, I would never attribute any negative quality to myself, but I'd be like, "Elaine, what are you doing?" And that's obviously—that's not positive, and I wouldn't say that to someone else if they were like doing something wrong; I wouldn't be like, "what are you doing?" but I do it to myself. And I never realized that until I actually started doing this. So, I think it's a good activity to start with to start thinking about, you know, how you talk to yourself. But I think as it goes on, it kinda gets a little repetitive. Where we're kind of just doing the same thing. So, I don't know like what else you could do to focus on self-compassion but in a different way.

Elaine felt the exercise was a helpful way to "realize" that she had not been talking to herself about her challenges as she would to a friend. However, after a while it became "a little repetitive," and she wanted opportunities "to focus on self-compassion but in a different way."

For Maria, the exercise may have felt incomplete because the prompt only asked these teachers to respond to challenges experienced *in their field placements*:

> Some things that affect what's going on in our experiences in our schools are obviously directly affected by things that are happening in our personal lives. And so, if this was 100% a private diary or something, all of those things would be like mixed together and you know, part of healing some of those things that happen in the school experience is going to be related to things that are happening in our personal life.

Maria's critique of the self-compassionate letter-writing exercise was that it focused only on her experiences in her field placement. As a result, Maria may have felt inauthentic separating her experiences in the field (as requested in the prompt) when what felt in need of self-compassion was often "mixed together" with experiences "related to things that are happening in [her] personal life."

These preservice teachers described their experiences practicing self-compassion through letter writing in complex ways when we spoke at the midpoint of their time in the teacher education program. While all of them felt it helped them address stress during the program and might protect them from burnout in the future, they also described other ways in which they felt the practice benefited them and their students. Furthermore, though they described to me its benefits, they also shared critiques of the letter-writing exercise. Again, these interviews took place halfway through their teacher education program, and even at this halfway point, they seemed to experience changes in the ease and benefits of this self-compassion practice. These changes and benefits also seemed to persist and evolve through the second half of their time in the teacher education program and into their first year as classroom teachers. In the following section, I explore how they recalled their experiences with self-compassion throughout their time in the teacher education program and how they believed these practices continued to impact them as first-year teachers.

Self-Compassion in the Past, Present, and Future

In the second round of semi-structured interviews with these former preservice teachers ($n=9$), which took place in June 2020, they reflected on their experiences with self-compassion throughout their time in the teacher education program. Additionally, several of them shared anecdotes about how their practice continued to evolve since becoming teachers, and how these practices impacted their students. Finally, many of them shared how they envisioned themselves continuing their self-compassion practice as classroom teachers moving forward. I share their reflections from the second round of semi-structured interviews by the four themes that emerged from my analysis:

1. Self-Compassion Helped and Should Have Happened More During the Teacher Education Program;
2. Self-Compassion Looked Different in the First Year of Teaching;
3. Being Self-Compassionate Impacts Students;
4. Critiques of Self-Compassionate Letter Writing Shifted in the First Year of Teaching.

Self-Compassion Helped and Should Have Happened More During the Teacher Education Program. All of the interviewed, former preservice teachers ($n=9$)

believed that taking time for self-compassionate letter writing during their 11 seminars over the course of their 3-semester teacher education program was important and that it helped them manage stress, feelings of inadequacy, and general challenges that they experienced in their field placements ($n = 9$). In fact, for some of them, their retrospective reflection on the practice illuminated the desire to have had more time for the letters and for other aspects of their teacher education program (e.g., coursework) to be more encouraging of self-compassion practice for them and the other preservice teachers enrolled in the program. Quinn explained:

> What I thought would have been helpful as well is being introduced to the topic [self-compassion] before starting the TEP. But I know that's hard, you know, to figure that out, because, dang, I definitely just saw a lot of my friends still being very critical of themselves all the time, and myself, you know, and sometimes that's just going to be part of it. You know? I'm just saying, I feel like knowing what I know now, it would definitely have been really cool to already [have] been practicing some of those, some of those ways of thinking before jumping into that professional world, you know what I mean?

Here, Quinn expressed that entering the teacher education program, not just her future classroom, already having self-compassion skills may have prevented her and her fellow preservice teachers from "still being very critical of themselves all the time" as they struggled with challenges throughout the program.

Nicole described having the time to write self-compassionate letters in her interview as "probably the best thing" about her time in the teacher education program. In fact, she wished, like Quinn, that self-compassion practice had been what she described as "the lead way" into the program:

> I think that was very important because I think it's a lot, it takes a toll on you to go to work and try to provide all this for the children and on top of yourself. So, I feel like that honestly should be the lead way into the TEP because if you're not spending the time to help yourself to make sure you're in a good place, I don't think you'll be prepared to help somebody else be in a good place, especially children. So for me, I think that needs to be the lead way. For sure.

It seemed to Nicole, that "to make sure" she was "in a good place" was necessary in order "to help somebody else be in a good place," and that, to her, writing these self-compassionate letters was a way to do that for herself and her students.

Maria, like Quinn and Nicole, also wished she had been allotted more time to write the letters, not leading up to their enrollment in the teacher education program as Quinn and Nicole described, but during the 11 times

I visited their seminars. In her second interview as a first-year teacher reflecting back on her experiences writing these letters, Maria said:

> I loved the activity itself. I think the only thing that was unfortunate was that it always had, had to be pushed into, you know, the last five minutes of class or the first five minutes. And so we're already all drained from class. And so I think that maybe that might've skewed whatever data you were getting from people [laughs], or their feelings towards it. I don't really know. So, the activity was wonderful, but it was just unfortunate.

I began this work knowing that time (Facchinetti, 2010) and workload (Chaplain, 2008) are common stressors for preservice teachers (Horgan et al., 2018), and though my efforts to create time for them to write their self-compassionate letters was my way of mitigating that stress, I did not account for the fact that they might still be "drained from class," as Maria described.

Bob, Anna, and Amy also described how important they felt it was to their development as preservice teachers—and now as classroom teachers—when we spoke during our second round of semi-structured interviews. Bob said:

> Okay. Oh my gosh. Firstly, I feel like it's changed my life. Entering the TEP, I wasn't very kind to myself. And then, you coming in and asking us to write these things—that felt cheesy at first—but then. . . . I found that that was kind of just how I spoke to myself like all the time. I'd be like, "Hey, you're doing fine, you're doing a good job." And I think that followed me throughout my whole experience in the TEP. Even now like I'll take a shower—that's when I'll talk to myself—I'll be like "you're doing a good job. It's okay. The world's crazy—you're doing a good job." I feel like everybody entering the TEP should do that. 'Cause I feel like I've benefited from it so much.

In Bob's first interview, she described how "interesting" it felt at first to write to herself in this way and that it got easier and began to benefit her by the midpoint of her enrollment in the teacher education program. Here, she remembered how "cheesy" the practice felt at first, but that ultimately, she "benefited from it so much." Additionally, Bob felt that the opportunity to practice self-compassion throughout the teacher education program should be available to other preservice teachers, too.

Anna described her feelings about writing the self-compassionate letters after graduating from the teacher education program:

> I think if we had not had the time for self-compassion, I would have never, maybe I would have, but I don't know if I would have established that idea early on that it's okay to talk to yourself the way, you know, you would want to talk to a friend; we're not really taught to do that. That's not something that you learn

in K through 12 and a lot of college students don't learn it, but it's really useful. 'Cause you're just like "I'm being too hard on myself" or, "Oh, well, yeah, I can change this. I can have higher expectations, but I did do this. I did do these things."

For Anna, having time to practice self-compassion in the teacher education program seemed to have "taught" her that "it's okay" to talk to herself "the way you would want to talk to a friend." As other participants reflected, and Neff and Germer (2018) expressed, many people are taught to be caring toward others but not necessarily to themselves. Anna's comments aligned with this notion when she said she may not have learned to speak to herself in this way because it's "not something that you learn in K through 12 and a lot of college students don't learn it."

Finally, Amy, like the others, described what she found to be most important about having time to write these letters during the teacher education program:

> It's hard to focus on being your best self when you're so hard on yourself for making those mistakes. And talking to myself like I was my friend really helped me to refocus and just feel like a better version of myself. . . . I would hate to think what the [teacher education program] would have been like without having those [self-compassionate letters] and being able to do those.

Like many of the participants in my study, Amy experienced many feelings of stress when it came to making mistakes that made her and the other former preservice teachers feel inadequate. She believed that having the opportunity to write these letters "helped her refocus and just feel like a better version of herself."

Because this second round of interviews happened six months after their graduation, they had not—to my knowledge—written any self-compassionate letters since their final seminar in the teacher education program. Despite this time gap, they maintained their belief that self-compassion practice mattered to them while they were learning to be teachers, and now that they were teachers.

Self-Compassion Looked Different in the First Year of Teaching. Selena reflected on what self-compassion looked like for her as a first-year teacher:

> I think it's helpful after experiencing the first parent blaming me for their child's behavior and after being hit and having things thrown at me and all of that, just taking that moment to understand this is the now and it's not the forever—what am I going to learn from today? What can I do tomorrow that won't necessarily change the situation but it will change my reaction? It's like taking those times to just sit and really think; that to me is how I do my self-compassion. Instead of

blaming myself and pointing the finger, I tell myself, "You know what? I didn't deserve that. It happened; now what am I going to do tomorrow?"

Here, Selena expressed that these practices changed the way she reacted toward herself in stressful and challenging situations that lasted into her first year of teaching. Additionally, she encouraged herself to find some positives in challenging moments because they might help her be more prepared "tomorrow."

Leslie described what self-compassion was like for her now as it pertains to the challenges she experienced as a first-year teacher:

> I would come home sometimes, and I would cry just because I was so tired and I would stay at school till like seven or eight at one point. And after that I was like, "You know what? I can't keep doing this." So, I made a promise to myself that I have to take care of me. And after that, I stay at school till . . . 4:30 and then I'm gone. 'Cause I'm like, that's too much. And if it gets done, it gets done. If not, then I'll do it tomorrow or something, you know, I'm like, I need time to rest. And that helps so much. So, I think just like taking, like making a promise to myself that I was gonna come home at a certain time, like that made a huge difference.

Leslie's "promise" to herself about taking care of herself and having boundaries with her work schedule may be an important way to prevent her from burning out and leaving teaching, as many other teachers have (Dunn, 2018; Ryan et al., 2017), particularly because not being able to take care of personal needs has been found to be a common source of teachers' stress (Kelly & Berthelsen, 1995). As Neff and Germer (2018) wrote, people who take care of others (e.g., nurses, mental health clinicians, and in this case, teachers) are often encouraged "to draw clear emotional boundaries between ourselves and those we care for" as a way to prevent burnout (p. 138), but this can be challenging to "the quality of the relationship" (p. 138) between the caregiver and the person being cared for. Leslie approached the drawing of this boundary not with the students she cared for as a teacher, but with her time and how she spent it outside of school. She believed such a boundary with her time would allow her to do her job effectively while simultaneously taking care of herself.

Amy's self-compassion practice also evolved in ways similar to Leslie's as a first-year teacher:

> I guess I'm doing self-compassion in different forms. Instead of talking to myself like I'm my friend, it's more like I choose myself. And when I'm having a rough time, I'm doing something I enjoy either to take my mind off it or to help me and feel better. Now it's a different form of compassion to myself. I'm no longer—it's not necessarily talking to myself, like in letters and letter form. When I think

about like my shortcomings—because I'm in an educational setting again, and I see my shortcomings as a teacher, they're less so. It's more just learning the routines of where I'm at and trying to do all that. I know I was hard on myself, even then I'm just like, "why am I so slow? Why can't I get what I'm supposed to do?" And then I saw that and I was like, "no, you shouldn't, you shouldn't be like that to yourself. That's not fair. There's only one of you, there's only so much you can do; just attack it another way another day. If you do forget, try to remind yourself."

Like Leslie, Amy described "choos[ing]" herself and making time for herself as a way to be self-compassionate as a first-year teacher. Interestingly, both Leslie and Amy's evolved approach to self-compassion seemed more aligned with notions of self-care, which often requires time to be set aside (Corey et al., 2018; Neff & Germer, 2018). However, Amy also described how she talked to herself with self-compassion as a first-year teacher when she would stop herself from being "hard on herself" for not "get[ting] what [she is] supposed to do" in her new teaching role. Amy was able to recognize when she was being self-critical and offer herself self-compassion as she learned these new routines and expectations (Neff, 2003, 2011; Neff & Germer, 2018).

Like the other former preservice teachers who were no longer writing letters and whose self-compassion practices had evolved, Anna's did too. In our second interview, Anna, who had just been offered a new teaching position, said:

So I've noticed since I graduated and moved back home I've been able to have this time to just kind of reflect a lot more. I mean, I don't usually write a lot of things down unless it's really weighing on me, but if I'm going through something or if I'm going through a challenge or struggle, I kind of do take that step back and I'm thinking, "okay, well what's really going on here? Why do I feel the way I do?" And just being aware of my emotions. I have done research on mindfulness meditation, so I think that has kind of added to the self-compassionate letters to myself. I feel like it really enhanced my experience.

In reviewing many of Anna's self-compassionate letters, excerpts of which are shared throughout this book, mindfulness was often the most pronounced of the three interacting components of self-compassion evident in her letters. Interestingly, her motivation to be mindful when "going through a challenge or struggle" was something she sustained through her own "research" and the mindful self-talk she—and these other former preservice teachers—described (Bishop et al., 2004; Kabat-Zinn, 1994; Neff & Germer, 2018; Siegel, 2010), even though she was no longer writing formal self-compassionate letters (to my knowledge). In addition to the ways these first-year teachers felt that self-compassion had mattered to them as preservice teachers and continued to matter to them as teachers, they also described the ways in which they felt being self-compassionate impacted their students.

Being Self-Compassionate Impacts Students. As preservice teachers, these now-teachers described some ways in which they felt practicing self-compassion through letter writing might impact their students when they became teachers. As first-year teachers, they described ways in which they felt being self-compassionate did *indeed* impact their students. For example, in our second interview, Quinn said:

> I think the number one thing about self-compassion that has been really helpful, not only in helping my own morale and my own mental well-being while teaching, has also been the fact that it really has affected the way that I treat students and the way that I encourage students to think about themselves, you know? I think it ties in really nicely with the growth mindset.

Carol Dweck is often credited with the concept of the growth mindset that Quinn mentioned. On this subject, Dweck wrote:

> This growth mindset is based on the belief that your basic qualities are things you can cultivate through your efforts. Although people may differ in every which way—in their initial talents and aptitudes, interests, or temperaments—everyone can change and grow through application and experience. (Dweck, 2012, p. 16)

By practicing self-compassion, Quinn experienced an additional benefit in her work with students; that she is encouraging them to have a growth mindset (Dweck, 2012, 2014) about their own challenges, just as Quinn was developing a growth mindset about herself through self-compassion.

Nicole also described how she felt being a self-compassionate teacher impacted her students:

> If you can't take it easy on yourself and you can't take the time to do something for yourself that calms you or puts you in a certain mindset, then I don't know how you're going to go through the day. . . . I want to make sure I provide an environment where [my students are] able to take time for themselves and make sure they know that's okay. Like if you need five minutes, take those five minutes, it's not the end of the world. If you come back ready to go, then I'm happy. If you're in a good place and I'm in a good place, we're ready to go. That's all I want. Because I feel like that's what basically social–emotional learning is all about—part of it is self-compassion. That's probably the biggest part of it all.

It seems that from Nicole's perspective, a part of getting "through the day" as a teacher and as a student is to get into a "mindset" that allows you to do so successfully, that to do this may require taking a few minutes, and "that's okay." From Nicole's perspective, having herself and her students feel they are "in a good place" is a prerequisite for successful teaching and learning to occur. Further, it appeared that Nicole believed that checking in with herself in this way—and having her students check in with themselves in this way—was a way to practice self-compassion, which she believed to be "the biggest part of" social–emotional learning.

Anna also expressed that modeling self-compassion to her students would encourage them to be more self-compassionate about their own challenges:

> Whenever I am stressed or when I feel like I am just overwhelmed with the amount of things that need to get done, just stopping and thinking, "okay, this is okay, let's look at what I've accomplished so far. I will get through it" and just talking to myself. Also, making sure that if I come across other people who are stressed or if my students are stressed, I can kind of give them the same kind of tool and be like, "okay, well what have you done? What have you done that you're proud of so far, what are you struggling with and how can we get you to where you need to go?"

Like Quinn, Anna believed that if students heard this kind of language modeled to them, it might encourage them to address—rather than avoid—those challenges (Dweck, 2012; Johnston, 2003). As Anna put it, it might encourage them to keep going to figure out "where [they] need to go." Like Nicole, Anna also felt that self-compassion connected to social–emotional learning and said later in the interview, "I know that it has a place in my classroom a hundred percent."

Although Quinn, Anna, and Nicole saw how being self-compassionate impacted their students and encouraged them to also be self-compassionate, Bob shared a powerful moment she experienced with a student in which she supported him directly in addressing his suffering with self-compassion:

> He was very upset one day that his parents had said something to him and it was pretty harsh. I'm not going to step in and be like, "your parents are wrong," I'm going to say, "Nope, sometimes people say things and you are allowed to disagree with what they're telling you." And I told him about self-compassion, and I basically told him to do what you asked us to do, but I told him to do it in a mirror looking at himself. I said, "Look in the mirror and just talk to yourself." And I was so surprised at how he responded to that, he genuinely was listening. And he genuinely was like, "okay." And I asked him "okay, what did I ask you to do?" And he walked me through it and gave me like goosebumps. I started crying. We were both crying—it was crazy.

Although the self-compassion practice Bob fostered for her student here was different than the practice she and the other former preservice teachers participated in (i.e., self-compassionate letter writing), the intention was the same. Rather than him being overwhelmed by feelings of inadequacy, Bob encouraged her student to talk to himself in the mirror like he was his own friend (Neff, 2011; Neff & Germer, 2018), just as Bob and the other participants did in their self-compassionate letters while enrolled in their teacher education program.

Critiques of Self-Compassionate Letter Writing Shifted in the First Year of Teaching. While enrolled in the teacher education program, the participants had some critiques of the self-compassionate letter writing. Mainly, that it was repetitive, that there should have been more time for it, and that the letters were only connected to challenges *in their field placements*. Although none of them mentioned in the second round of interviews as first-year teachers that they wished the practice was more inclusive of challenges outside of their field placements or that they had more time to write their letters during their seminars, two of these first-year teachers reflected back on their experiences with the letter-writing exercise and found purpose in the exercise being repetitive. For example, Leslie said:

> I loved the writing prompts and everything like that. I think just even though it was the same thing every time, I think that the power of it was that you have to think of something new every time. And just to remind yourself that, you know, you can always talk. . . . I don't know how to explain it, but you can always have something good to say about yourself and have something to be proud of.

For Leslie, it seemed that the letter-writing prompt being "the same thing every time" gave her the opportunity to find "something to be proud of" in the challenges she experienced as a preservice teacher that she could respond to with self-compassion. Bob also felt that continuing to participate in the self-compassionate letter-writing was important for her despite it being repetitive:

> I think the good thing is that I kept doing it, but in the moment it didn't feel like it was helping very much. But then, after looking back I'm like, "Oh my goodness, that really helped me and it shaped me into who I am right now" even though it didn't feel like it was helping. So, I think just sneak it into people's systems and it'll just help them without them even realizing.

It seemed that Bob and Leslie felt that the self-compassionate letter-writing exercise was repetitive, but that this may have been "the power of it," as Leslie described, or a way that the exercise helped Bob "without . . . even realizing." Either way, and for at least these two former preservice teachers, the repetition that was critiqued at the midpoint of the teacher education program was remembered as being useful.

Field Supervisors and Cohort Coordinators' Impressions of Self-Compassion

For confidentiality reasons, the cohort coordinators ($n=2$) and field supervisors ($n=5$) did not know which of the preservice teachers were involved in this study. Nana, the cohort coordinator for this cohort of preservice teachers, was the only person other than me who was present during the seminars while they wrote their letters. Because these were Nana's seminars, all preservice teachers in her cohort—regardless of their participation in this study—did the exercise as part of the "work" of the first 10 minutes of the seminars, but only those who signed consent forms had their letters analyzed in this study. Although Nana and the field supervisors did not have knowledge of how these preservice teachers responded to their experiences with challenges, stressors, and feelings of inadequacy with self-compassion, according to Nana and the field supervisors, they believed such practices would be useful for preservice teachers in the teacher education program, particularly when it came to addressing their stress as future teachers and how they went about establishing classroom community.

Self-Compassion Practice Could Reduce Stress and Burnout. In my interview with Nana, she reflected on how she saw these preservice teachers experience the self-compassionate letter-writing exercise:

> I will tell you that they loved having your presence over the course of the three semesters. They really looked forward to, to your time with them. It was almost like I could feel a big breath in and breath out sigh for them to throw all their worries away and write their self-compassionate letter. So, I thought that was a very, very positive aspect of having you part of the group.

In addition to finding the exercise useful for these preservice teachers, for Nana, part of what made the exercise feel like an opportunity to "throw all their worries away" was that I came in person to their seminars. Nana went on to explain ways she adapted another assignment for future cohorts after our work together concluded to encourage the preservice teachers she works with to be more self-compassionate about moments in which they felt unsuccessful in their field placements:

> I think it was a very useful exercise. In fact, I've kept that as my journal piece. "I felt successful when and I felt unsuccessful when." Every person is individualized. I know that you've read their journals, and so some people are like totally so reflective and write a big piece. And then some people would write one sentence. . . . I think the actual "I felt successful and I felt unsuccessful" actually gave them just a sentence frame to look at their whole week and it wasn't as

> overwhelming as everything else that they had to reflect on. . . . In fact, I would be interested to see how many students maybe started with the "I felt unsuccessful" first. And then went back and did the "I felt successful"—because I think educators as a group are very hard on themselves.

Here, Nana expressed the importance of reflecting weekly on things that went well ("I felt successful") and things that did not go well ("I felt unsuccessful") for the preservice teachers she supported. Further, it appeared that Nana was considering how a preservice teacher might approach this journaling by starting with what "felt unsuccessful first" because of her belief that "educators as a group are very hard on themselves." Taken together, Nana believed participating in self-compassion practice was important enough that she wanted to carry forward aspects of the practice in her journal assignments and that she saw this as important because of how self-critical ("hard on themselves") she believes teachers can be.

Susan, a field supervisor, also reflected on the potential impact of incorporating self-compassion with preservice teachers to address stress before they became classroom teachers:

> It's so hard to be a teacher! So hard; it's so stressful. And I think, I mean I know a lot of people get into it and then they quit. They're like, "I can't, I just can't do it." And a lot of it has to do with that we are not taught to stop and to care for ourselves and to take a break. To not worry about the kids in the shower at five o'clock in the morning. You know? I'll be up until 11 o'clock, you know, trying to figure out, you know, write some plan that tomorrow won't even go the way that you planned it the night before, you know what I mean? I think too that we want to be perfect. We want to do it right. We don't want to make a mistake or teach the wrong thing. I feel like the TEP is kind of where you can open it up to be like, "it's okay to make a mistake. It's okay to be human." And it's OK to take the time and say "I'm exhausted."

Susan's reflections here make clear her belief in what other researchers are beginning to find: Teaching is a stressful occupation, and that stress is leading teachers to leave the profession (Dunn, 2018; Ryan et al., 2017). Further, as I stated earlier, how teachers relate to the stressors of teaching begins in their teacher education program (Gold, 1985; Horgan et al., 2018), which Susan believed is where preservice teachers can learn to be "open" to making "a mistake" and learn "[i]t's okay to be human." Taken together, centering such practices in teacher education programs may be a way to reduce feelings of stress and burnout among pre- and inservice teachers.

Susan continued to discuss more specifically what prioritizing self-compassion and self-care in schools could do for students enrolled in teacher education programs when they become teachers:

> I wish that districts took it more seriously and did things on self-care and self-compassion and easing up on the pressures that teachers feel; I just, I think it would be great. I think it would be beneficial. I think we could send some, a bunch of people out into education that care about themselves as much as they care about children, because I think that's missing sometimes. I think that the, um, burnout rate would go down. I really do, because I really think that, um, teaching is a calling for most people but the stress of it is not. I mean, nobody wants to go to work and cry, and that happens all the time. Teachers sitting in the parking lot at six o'clock in the morning crying before they have to go in and, you know, put on, put on the face and, and be perfect. So, for schools and for districts and stuff, I do think that, um, it could help with, I would hope that it would help with retention with keeping good teachers.

Here, Susan expressed that in order for teachers to be able to sufficiently address the stress they experience that may lead to burnout would require school districts to take self-compassion "more seriously" and provide opportunities for teachers to engage in self-compassion and self-care. She described her belief that to prioritize these practices would reduce burnout and attrition among teachers, which has been shown to be true among professional caregivers (e.g., Neff & Germer, 2018).

Another field supervisor, Alex, spoke during our interview about how prioritizing self-compassion practice in teacher education programs may be beneficial to future teachers:

> Teaching is such an under-respected job and everyone is so overly critical of us. You could potentially go like a month as a teacher without hearing any good. Because the world is so critical on you as a teacher, I feel like you can kind of pick up on that behavior. It is so easy to just like have one bad moment and that's the end of your day, or maybe rippled into really messing with the rest of your day. But no, like teachers need therapy. That should be a thing, you know, teachers need therapy because there's just so much to unpack because you're dealing with so many humans. So I feel like self-compassion is a form of it. Like, you know, like sitting down and journaling, that's a form of therapy. . . . Teachers need to like release all the criticism they face and talk about the really terrible circumstances they're under in order to do their job. Because I know for me, if I bottled up all my feelings when I was a teacher, I was just kinda like "fuck everybody, I don't even want to do this job."

Alex candidly described in the above what researchers have found to be causing teachers to feel significant work-related stress (Adams, 2013; Chang, 2009; Simos, 2013; Yong & Yue, 2007), particularly the challenges related to "dealing with so many humans" (i.e., students) and feeling criticized by others (Yong & Yue, 2007) that have led to burnout and attrition (Ryan et al., 2017).

Clare, a field supervisor, reflected on the experience of one preservice teacher she worked with who expressed directly to Clare how she felt she benefited from having time to write the self-compassionate letters during her seminars:

> She was one of the ones that I remember pretty clearly saying that she really found the self-compassionate writing to be really valuable, that it was something that she really enjoyed doing, and that it was really helpful to her to be thinking about herself and her work in that way. She was one of the ones that tended to be super prepared as a means to avoid making mistakes. I think that the self-compassionate practices helped her in a sense to sort of be okay with the idea that she might have made a mistake without it being so scary or terrible or any of those things that, you know, when you think you've made a mistake and it seems like life is over. So I was happy to hear that this seemed to be having some impact on at least some students, but also happy for her that it was a way for her to find some comfort and to allow herself to be in a little bit of a different place than she was before.

From Clare's perspective, the opportunity to write the self-compassionate letters helped "at least" one student "be in a little bit of a different place than she was before" when it came to becoming more comfortable making mistakes in her field placements. Clare's comments about mistakes feeling "scary or terrible" also align with the ways in which these preservice teachers described how making mistakes made them feel like they were not teachers or that others did not see them as a teacher. Furthermore, as Neff and Germer (2018) wrote, self-compassion develops within practitioners a deepened sense of common humanity—one of the interconnected components of self-compassion—by bringing awareness to the fact that "[w]e fall into the trap of believing that things are 'supposed' to go well and that something has gone wrong when they don't. Of course, it's highly likely—in fact, inevitable—that we'll make mistakes and experience hardships on a regular basis. This is completely normal and natural" (pp. 10–11). Clare expressed that for this preservice teacher in particular, the opportunity to relate to her mistakes with self-compassion and normalize her mistakes made the act of making mistakes less "scary" and "terrible."

Self-Compassion Could Help Establish Strong Classroom Communities. In addition to seeing benefits from practicing self-compassion for these preservice teachers when it came to their own mental health, a field supervisor (Susan) and cohort coordinator (Nana) I interviewed for this study also felt these practices would have an impact on students and classroom communities. Nana and Susan thought these preservice teachers benefited from practicing self-compassion in this teacher education program, that teachers would benefit from practicing self-compassion, and that doing so would reduce

burnout and turnover. They also expressed that these practices could impact how students would relate to their own challenges, stressors, and feelings of inadequacy. For example, Nana said:

> I hope that these PSTs [preservice teachers] take forward with them the whole idea that mistakes are learning opportunities. And that if they can understand that kids behave in a way that's expressing their needs and look at the need rather than the actual behavior—and really think about natural consequences rather than punishment—then they'll practice self-compassion when they're using language with kids such as, "okay, you made a mistake. How can we fix the mistake?" You know? "How can we shrink the problem and not stretch the problem?" "How can we move on? What have we learned from this?"

Here, Nana expressed what Clare described about self-compassion practice being a way to reframe reactions to the mistakes these preservice teachers made. Nana took this a step further by pondering how they could use that same self-compassionate language to support their students to also realize that mistakes are learning opportunities, that mistakes are inevitable, and that mistakes do not need to be avoided. Taken together, Nana believed that learning to utilize language reflective of a growth mindset (Dweck, 2012) about themselves and their own teaching mistakes (Dweck, 2014) might also encourage preservice teachers to model similar language as classroom teachers when their students make mistakes.

Nana went on to say she wondered if these practices with students would encourage these former preservice teachers' students to become self-compassionate as well:

> How many self-compassionate teachers does a child need to carry that on in their own persona? I think depending on the school that you're in, you may or may not have a lot of exposure to people who think that way. If we can hope that each child has at least one or two self-compassionate adults that are around them, then I think that we can hope that the seed has been planted.

Nana believed that the climate of a school might dictate whether or not teachers "think [in a self-compassionate] way" and that "exposure" to "at least one or two self-compassionate adults" would be an important factor in whether or not the self-compassion "seed has been planted" within children.

Susan (a field supervisor), like Nana in the above, also reflected on what it could mean for students and classroom communities to be led by a self-compassionate teacher:

> If you have a teacher that cares about herself and takes care of herself, I think it makes the community in the classroom more caring and compassionate because that's what the teacher can model for the kids. . . . You know, we're all guilty

of during any sort of testing thing or high stress thing, being extra hard on the kids too, which then makes us feel bad. I mean, it's just like this vicious circle of everybody feeling bad and then not knowing how to deal with it.

Neoliberal reforms in schools like high-stakes tests are often reported by teachers as being stressful, and for some, a rationale to leave the classroom altogether (Dunn, 2018). Susan believed that "testing . . . or high stress" parts of the school year lead to "everybody feeling bad" but that these feelings could be avoided if a teacher "care[d] about herself . . . [and] model[ed] that for the kids."

Both Nana and Susan saw great value in having opportunities for these preservice teachers to practice self-compassion for several reasons, ranging from how they dealt with stress in the here and now as preservice teachers, to how becoming a self-compassionate teacher could prevent them from burning out and turning over when they are teaching in their own classrooms. Further, they expressed that modeling self-compassionate language to their students could encourage teachers and students to develop a growth mindset (Dweck, 2012) about themselves.

The Impact of Identity

There were three moments in the interviews I conducted with the preservice teachers, the cohort coordinators, and field supervisors in which the person I interviewed mentioned the ways a preservice teacher's racial identity impacted their experience in this teacher education program. Given that this was a diverse pool of preservice teachers, with the majority of interviewed identifying as women of color (interview 1: $n = 7$ of 10, interview 2: $n = 6$ of 9), this was quite surprising to me given the extant research on how racial identity can impact a preservice teacher's experience in a teacher education program (e.g., Amos, 2010; Gomez & Rodriguez, 2011; Kohli, 2008; Sheets & Chew, 2002; Weisman & Hansen, 2008). In retrospect, I wonder if this limitation may have to do with the particular questions I asked as a researcher, the particular sources of data I collected, and my own positionality. Although I did not ask explicitly in our interviews how their racial identity impacted their experiences in the teacher educator program, Selena, who identified as Hispanic, described a moment in which one of her teacher educators made incorrect assumptions about how she experienced her identity. Here, I share what she told me in our second interview, when she was a first-year teacher:

> I had some professors in the TEP, you know, that would preach diversity and preach equality and equity, but were very stereotypical on who I am or who I would be as a teacher because I was Hispanic. So, it was very hypocritical. And you know, some of the backhanded comments that I would be given from

an assignment or even through a discussion were just really frustrating for me to navigate through that space. And then, even like trying to take the time to educate others on it. So, there was one example in the reading class with my professor. I said, "You know, I haven't really read a book about myself and I'm looking for one. I just don't know what it looks like." And she brings me *Esperanza Rising*. And I look at her and I was like, "My dad's not a drug dealer, I'm not running away from Mexico to not be married to my uncle. That is ridiculous. Both of my parents are educated. They work in the education field as administrators. My mom was getting the doctoral degree. What makes you think that this is my story? I don't even know Spanish because my parents were taught that that was bad. So what was I taught? that Spanish was bad. I'm here trying to navigate through a space where I'm too Mexican for White people and too White for the Mexican people, and trying make a name of who I am and who my generation of Latinas are because it's a lot of our story." And she kind of looked at me with this blank face and I told her "that's very typical of you. How you can do that?"

While Selena was the only preservice teacher who expressed an experience with racism in the teacher education program to me in our interviews, hers was not an uncommon experience among preservice teachers of color. For example, Selena wanted an opportunity to see herself reflected in literature to "extend" her sociocultural knowledge, but her course instructor was not prepared to provide her appropriate literature that could do that (Amos, 2010; Weisman & Hansen, 2008). Instead, her instructor made a stereotypical assumption about Selena, her identity, and her experiences. Although Selena was compelled to respond to this instructor about this assumption, many preservice teachers of color remain silent after having similar experiences in which their attempts at educating others by sharing their sociocultural knowledge are met with "retaliation and ostracism" (Amos, 2010, p. 36). Finally, while Selena felt this teacher education program attempted to "preach diversity and preach equality and equity," her own experiences in it told a different story.

Alex, a field supervisor who identified as a "Black gay woman," described the way in which she saw preservice teachers of color experience the teacher education program differently than their White peers:

> With the PSTs of color, I felt more of a sense of urgency, I would say. I'm thinking about like one girl in particular who was just on every deadline. She was very organized; she never missed a day. I would always find myself wanting to check in on her because I didn't want her to feel like the school was exploiting her because I felt that most of the PSTs were at straight up predominantly White schools; I had a lot of thoughts about that. But anyway, she worked really hard and she never missed a day. I believe only one person of color missed a day out of that cohort and it was Nora, and it was because she actually had strep throat.

> So, it was interesting to me to see like the differences, because I felt like some of them were prioritizing like their social life. Like for me, I have a lot of thoughts. I feel like people exploit teachers, I feel like teachers are overworked and underpaid, right? And I feel like people don't look at teachers as human. So, they want them to come in when they're sick, they want them to do all these crazy things. But at the same time, I felt like a tension at times, because as a Black teacher I always was just like, "this is important to me" like there was a sense of urgency behind it. And my mom just kind of always ingrained in me that work is important and you're not gonna miss it unless you're going to the hospital.

There is a lot to unpack in Alex's comments, and what follows are my best attempts at doing so given my own positionality, aware that I missed nuance because of my own identity. To begin, Alex's comments seem to resonate with research from Ladson-Billings (1991), Dingus (2008), Sleeter (2001), Amos (2010), and others that found teachers of color to have an elevated commitment to the work they did as teachers, namely to the success of marginalized children. Alex expressed in her statements a concern for this student being exploited as a result of her commitment to her work with students in a school setting with mostly White teachers who Alex was concerned may be taking advantage of this preservice teacher's work ethic. Although Alex and I were not able to unpack this further, her concluding comments about her own work ethic inspired by her mother may be connected to what previous researchers have found; that despite a heightened commitment to the success of marginalized children in schools (Achinstein et al., 2010, p. 85; Su, 1997; Villegas & Irvine, 2009), "the professional competency of Black women teachers [is] constantly under question" (Achinstein et al., 2010, p. 373).

Maggie, a cohort coordinator, also expressed concerns about how preservice teachers of color experienced the field placement component of the teacher education program:

> You know what struck me as concerning? I remember having a student who grew up in this area, and she said to me, "Maggie, I can never teach in a wealthier school or district. I just can't." And I said, "why?" And she said, "I just, just don't feel I'll fit in. I need to go back to this part of the city to teach." And it broke my heart. It really did. And then she shared later on and it was more her family. As a young Black woman, her father felt it was best that she stayed within her community and would not have been accepted [at a predominantly White school]. And that really was hard to hear, but I understand, and I have to respect that. I've had it with this group and those that felt that "my CT didn't like me because I am not White like her."

As researchers have found that a preservice teacher's relationship with their cooperating teacher has a significant impact on how stressful their experience in a teacher education program will be (Murray-Harvey et al., 2000), Maggie shared an additional concern that preservice teachers of color could be matched with a potentially racist cooperating teacher in a predominantly White school. From Alex and Maggie's perspective, such a match could deepen experiences with stress connected to a perceived negative relationship between preservice teachers of color and their White cooperating teachers. Here, Maggie appeared to be highly attuned to how race and racism impact a preservice teacher's experience in a teacher education program, which may be further complicated by the ways in which Whiteness is privileged in schools and teacher education programs (Amos, 2010; Gomez & Rodriguez, 2011; Kohli, 2008; Sheets & Chew, 2002; Weisman & Hansen, 2008).

Self-Compassion Scale Statistical Analysis

In addition to learning about how practicing self-compassion seemed to impact these preservice teachers from the perspectives of their cohort coordinators, field supervisors, and their own written and verbal reflections of their personal experiences with self-compassion, these preservice teachers also completed Neff's Self-Compassion Scale: Short Form (Raes et al., 2011) once each semester while enrolled in the 3-semester teacher education program. I was curious to see quantitatively how their ratings of self-compassion might change over the course of their enrollment in this program, perhaps as a result of participating in the self-compassionate letter-writing exercise.

Quantitative analysis and descriptive statistics (see Appendix B) indicated that the preservice teachers in this study experienced changes in their mean self-compassion ratings over time, increasing from semester 1 (2.95 out of 5) to semester 2 (3.27 out of 5), and from semester 3 to semester 4 (3.54 out of 5). In fact, paired-sample t-tests indicate that their scores increased significantly, with a with a p value of .018 and a large Cohen's d effect size of .76 from semester 2 to semester 3, and a p value of .013 and a large Cohen's d effect size of .77 from semester 1 to semester 3 (see Appendix B). There was no significant increase in their ratings of self-compassion between semesters 1 and 2. It should be noted that though each preservice teacher received Neff's Self-Compassion Scale: Short Form (Raes, 2011) once each semester, not everyone completed the scale each time. To accommodate this in my analysis, missing values were flagged in SPSS so that they were not used to calculate means or impact the results of the t-tests.

Such an increase is highly correlated with high job satisfaction (Barnard & Curry, 2012) and reductions in feelings of stress, empathy fatigue, and burnout among professional caregivers (e.g., Neff et al., 2020). This finding mirrors other studies that indicate self-compassion practices can significantly increase one's self-compassion scores over time (e.g., Neff & Germer, 2013; Neff & Germer, 2018).

Discussion

These research findings illuminate how these preservice teachers experienced the self-compassionate letter-writing exercise, and how they and their field supervisors and cohort coordinators felt the practice could help them manage stress, challenges, and feelings of inadequacy in their field placements over the course of their 3-semester teacher education program and in the future as teachers. Although some of the preservice teachers expressed that the practice was repetitive when we spoke at the midpoint of the teacher education program, in speaking with them again as first-year teachers, some felt the repetition made the practice effective. Having the opportunity to practice self-compassion and write to themselves like a good friend softened the ways in which they experienced stress during their development as teachers. Additionally, their self-compassion scores increased significantly over their time in the teacher education program to a mean that is on par with professional caregivers who experience "compassion satisfaction" in their work as caregivers, fewer instances of burnout and empathy fatigue, and increases in job satisfaction (Barnard & Curry, 2012; Delaney, 2018; Duarte et al., 2016; Eriksson et al., 2018; Finlay-Jones et al., 2015; Knier et al., 2020; Neff et al., 2020; Stebnicki, 2015; Yela et al., 2019).

The cohort coordinators and field supervisors did not have much insight into the self-compassionate letter-writing intervention I did with the preservice teachers; however, they believed it would be beneficial for teachers and preservice teachers to practice self-compassion. In fact, the benefits they imagined were quite similar to the benefits the preservice teachers in this study experienced (e.g., feeling that mistakes are learning experiences). Furthermore, these former preservice teachers and their former cohort coordinators and field supervisors expressed that these practices could and did change the ways in which they interacted with their students (e.g., being more mindful during stressful interactions) and would encourage their young students to relate to their own experiences with stress, challenges, and inadequacy with a self-compassionate growth mindset (Dweck, 2012). The field supervisors and cohort coordinators also described how self-critical they believed teachers can be and how certain aspects of their work (e.g., testing, being criticized by others) seemed to amplify stress that can lead to intense instances of self-critique (Dunn, 2018) and how that can impact a teacher's relationship with their students. While these former preservice teachers may not yet have been aware of some of these challenges because they were only a few months into their first year of teaching, according to their cohort coordinators and field supervisors, such self-compassionate practices may help support them during these heightened moments of job-related stress in ways similar to professional caregivers (Neff & Germer, 2018).

Conclusion and What's Next

Now that you've learned about the empirical evidence pointing to the benefits of self-compassion practice among preservice and first-year teachers, it's time to get into the "meat" of this book. The chapters that follow are organized into four specific challenges I learned about from the preservice teachers in my dissertation study:

1. Delivering Academic Content to Students;
2. Meeting Students' Social, Emotional, and Behavioral Needs;
3. Relationship Dynamics with Cooperating Teachers, School Staff, Families, and Teacher Educators;
4. Life Outside the Classroom.

I open each chapter with a vignette from my own experience as a preservice teacher and first-year teacher who experienced each of these challenges many times in a variety of ways. Then I share what I learned from the preservice and first-year teachers I worked with in my study about how they experienced each challenge and how they responded to it with self-compassion.

Next, at the end of these chapters, I share a self-compassion prompt that you, the reader, can engage in to address each challenge with self-compassion. Then I share my own responses to each prompt in response to each chapter's opening vignette. Finally, I encourage you to complete Neff's Self-Compassion Scale: Short Form (Raes et al., 2011) (Appendix A) as you engage with the self-compassionate letter-writing prompts included throughout the book.

If you see your own experiences reflected in the challenges these preservice teachers and I shared in these chapters, may the process of reading about our experiences with stress give you a sense of common humanity—that these stressors are experienced by many preservice teachers, not just you. May the mindfulness that we demonstrate when we attempt to see the big picture—not just our mistakes—help you be more mindful of your own inevitable teaching mistakes and challenges. May the self-kindness with which we respond to these challenges inspire you to be more self-kind as these stressors present themselves.

CHAPTER 3

The Stress of Delivering Academic Content to Students

> The Hibernation Lesson That "Kind of Sucked"
> (Author's Student Teaching Journal, 1/25/2007)
>
> So, the [make your own] "what animals hibernate/where animals hibernate [counting book]" lesson I did today kind of sucked for my AM [i.e., morning] kids. They got that the numbers [on the pages] were supposed to go up and were able to guess the number of animals per page, as well as match the environments to the animals, but I felt that they weren't given the time to grasp it and got completely distracted. They would constantly flip ahead through the other pages and got lost really easily. I ended up getting almost snappy with a girl that kept asking to be in my group before it was her turn because she wouldn't stop. Luckily, I didn't, but I still felt mean. :(
>
> I revised for the PM [i.e., afternoon] kids and only gave out one sheet at a time and had them flip it over when they were done so I could give them a new one. Also, instead of having five kids per group like I did for AM, I just had four. Only one of the groups got kind of antsy, and when I felt they got the concept (after three [pages]), I told them they were finished and felt they had done enough. That was my lesson for the day → know when to sense when enough is enough and things won't be meaningful anymore.

I still remember how long it took me to prepare that hibernating counting book project for my students. I hand-drew hibernating frogs, bears, and chipmunks that were all cut out and ready to be counted and glued onto color-printed photos of collages I'd made of each animal's corresponding hibernation habitat. When the children in the AM pre-K class weren't "getting" it, I remember feeling so frustrated that I'd put all this time into an activity that wasn't really working. I felt like I was failing at teaching this academic content to my students and all the effort I'd put into it was for nothing.

However, the literature is clear: It takes time to be an effective teacher, and a huge component of being an effective teacher is delivering academic content (Darling-Hammond, 2000). Believing it possible to walk into your student teaching experience or your first classroom as a new teacher with all the skills and tricks that a veteran teacher possesses is therefore not a realistic or fair expectation of yourself. Instead of being harsh with yourself about the mistakes you make as a developing teacher, try thinking of those mistakes more like *required steps* that you have to take in order to be able to teach content effectively. When you can begin to see these steps (i.e., mistakes made when learning to teach academic content) as necessary to your development as a teacher, simply because they are unavoidable, their power to trigger negative feelings about your self-worth may diminish.

Imagine a toddler learning to walk. How much experimentation with crawling, cruising, coordination, and so on needs to happen before they can walk independently? How many tumbles and crashes before they learn to put all the different pieces together and ambulate? If you've ever been present when a toddler is learning to walk, how did their caregivers respond to the mistakes they made? Did they yell at them when they fell, or did they praise their effort? Did they expect them to be born walking, or did they understand that developing this skill takes time, effort, experimentation, and countless errors (and hours) to master? I would be highly concerned if a toddler's caregiver(s) expected them to be walking right away rather than praising their efforts. I would be even more concerned if they scolded their toddler when they fell over as they acquired the balance skills needed to walk. Why, then, should you—a new or developing teacher—have any expectation that you can skip over all the trips, stumbles, and crashes (hopefully metaphorical) when we know that they are just part of learning to be an effective teacher?

Like learning to walk (or any other skill that requires time to develop), you can't just skip to the end and be an effective teacher right away. It's a developmental process that requires time, coordinating multiple skills, and is marked by milestones and countless errors. But with time, the errors occur with less frequency. The mistakes become familiar, and we learn how to pick ourselves back up again. We even learn to anticipate the errors we made previously while teaching so we can begin to avoid them; and finally, our teaching moves seem to become second nature. That said, even when we have mastered a skill, mistakes still happen—that's just being human. World-class bakers make a buttercream that splits on occasion, Olympic gymnasts will occasionally fall off of balance beams, and the best teachers are tested with new challenges that they fail at from time to time.

MY OWN CHALLENGES DELIVERING ACADEMIC CONTENT AS A PRESERVICE TEACHER

In the summer of 2021, I moved from Austin, TX, to West Chester, PA, to begin a tenure-track position at West Chester University after completing my PhD at the University of Texas at Austin. Moving is always stressful, but one positive I lean into when moving is the opportunity to purge "stuff" while packing. In this particular moving purge, I came across my student teaching journal (see entry at the beginning of this chapter!) from my senior year of college. It's a spiral-bound, one-subject notebook that I filled with all kinds of experiences I had while student teaching in the spring of 2007.

At that time, my undergraduate institution—and I believe the Massachusetts Department of Education—required students seeking an early childhood teaching license (pre-K through grade 2 with and without disabilities) to have a divided student teaching semester: the first 5 weeks would be in either a pre-K or kindergarten classroom, and the remaining 10 weeks would be either in a 1st- or 2nd-grade classroom. For my student teaching experience, I was assigned to a pre-K classroom in Brockton, MA, for my first 5 weeks and a 2nd grade in Brockton, MA, for my final 10 weeks.

As I sat down to read my student teacher journal, I saw the preservice teachers from my dissertation research that guides this book clearly reflected in the challenges I experienced, even though our preservice teacher education experiences were separated by over a decade. It was amazing how clearly some of these memories came back while reading through my journal and how instantly empathetic I felt toward all preservice teachers when all of these old feelings of inadequacy came bubbling to the surface.

It's amazing to me how clearly I remember some of my biggest experiences with stress from that first year of teaching after all of these years. It feels a bit strange to be publishing the thoughts I had as a 22-year-old student teacher and first-year teacher, but I am hopeful that being vulnerable in this way as an author and researcher will inspire you to be vulnerable as you explore your own experiences with feelings of inadequacy while learning to be a teacher.

Before you read the rest of this chapter, take a moment to flip to Appendix A and complete Neff's Self-Compassion Scale: Short Form (Raes et al., 2011). Complete it honestly, and follow the directions to find your mean (average) self-compassion score. If you find that score is lower than you thought, please don't feel discouraged. As Neff and Germer (2018) found, practicing self-compassion regularly can increase your self-compassion score.

Further, if you are like the preservice teachers in my study, you may experience a significant increase in your self-compassion score by completing self-compassion exercises regularly like Neff's (2011) "exploring self-compassion through letter writing" (Barry, 2021, 2022, 2023) or the prompts I've adapted for this book to match the specific stressors that I've learned new and developing teachers experience through my research.

WHY IS DELIVERING ACADEMIC CONTENT TO STUDENTS STRESSFUL FOR PRESERVICE TEACHERS?

Throughout their enrollment in the teacher education program, the preservice teachers in my dissertation study described some of their most challenging, stressful, and unsuccessful moments in their field placements as the moments in which they did not feel successful teaching academic content to the students in their field placements. Although previous research on preservice teachers' experiences with stress is extremely limited (Horgan et al., 2018), the research that does exist illuminates that a source of stress for preservice teachers is the disconnect when they "have broad theoretical knowledge but are challenged when faced with real situations" (Onchwari, 2010, p. 392).

For the preservice teachers that I worked with in my study—and now as a teacher educator—it seemed that this disconnect illuminated by Onchwari (2010) and others (e.g., Darling-Hammond et al., 2000; Early & Winton, 2001; McCann & Johannessen, 2004) was also the case. While they had several courses connected to becoming teachers before beginning their formal enrollment in the teacher education program, their practical experiences with children in classrooms were the last three semesters of college with one field placement in a public elementary school for each of those 3 semesters. Their unsuccessful attempts at applying what they learned in coursework in their field placements seemed to be a consistent source of stress. Quinn described one such experience in her fieldwork journal:

> On Wednesday, my CT [cooperating teacher] asked me to lead the morning meeting very spontaneously. I accepted, and it went well until we got to the portion where we play a game. I could not for the life of me remember any of the games we played, my mind blanked. My CT stepped in and led that portion. It made me feel a little annoyed with myself since I had played [these] games countless times. I think I need more practice with situations where you have to think on your feet and don't have something planned out.

For Quinn, the application of what she was learning from her cooperating teacher left her feeling unsuccessful when having to "think on [her] feet"—a skill she believed could only be developed with "more practice" in real "situations," which is similar to findings from previous research (Darling-Hammond et al., 2000; Early & Winton, 2001; McCann & Johannessen, 2004; Onchwari, 2010).

Another stressor these preservice teachers experienced when it came to teaching academic content to the students in their field placements were when their lessons did not go as planned. In Elaine's fieldwork journal, she shared an experience emblematic of this phenomenon:

> This week I felt unsuccessful when I began teaching my Lit[erature] Unit on Tuesday. First, I had to change my initial plan because my CT introduced poems to them, so I had to come up with an engaging review activity, which I didn't. Second, my CT decided that she wanted me to teach all morning, which is fine, but I didn't get fair warning and I was teaching a new concept (the difference between using -ck, -k, and -ic). We had been doing the same word study

but with the ending sound [shun], but I had only ever reviewed it with them. After I taught that morning, I felt pretty incapable of teaching. Somewhere in the middle of the lesson, my CT had to step in and explain the concept better. I also had to work with a small reading group from a teacher workbook I had only read that morning. It was just a lot of new things and I was not ready for it.

Facchinetti (2010) found that "managing a crowded curriculum" (in Horgan et al., 2018, p. 218) was a common source of stress for preservice educators, and it seemed that for Elaine, her literature unit could not go on as planned given the amount of content her cooperating teacher was expected to teach her students. Further, feeling she "didn't get fair warning" from her cooperating teacher about teaching a new concept and then needing to "step in and explain the concept better" made Elaine feel "pretty incapable of teaching." This may also have put a strain on her relationship with her cooperating teacher, which researchers have found increases experiences of stress among preservice teachers (Murray-Harvey et al., 2000).

Amy wrote in her fieldwork journal about a similar challenge teaching her literature unit:

> I started my literature unit during station time, knowing the time would be reduced to just 20 minutes. We did not finish the story, and I did not get to ask the questions I wanted to. We will be revisiting the story a week later, so I feel much of my time was not used as well as it could have been.

Amy's challenge teaching her literature unit to her field students was tied to not completing what she'd planned to teach. Like Elaine, dealing with a crowded curriculum (Facchinetti, 2010) and subsequently needing to reduce her lesson time to 20 minutes created stress and made it challenging to feel like an effective teacher when things did not go as planned. Facchinetti (2010) also found that preservice teachers experienced stress related to time management, which also seemed to have impacted Amy's experience feeling unsuccessful in teaching her students effectively (i.e., not covering the content she planned to).

In the moments described previously, these preservice teachers seemed aware that things had not gone well (e.g., running out of time, not feeling prepared). In other instances, they reflected on challenges they experienced in which they did not realize they had been ineffective at teaching their students academic content until later on (e.g., after an assessment). Quinn wrote, "I thought a math lesson I taught went well, but then students' assessments showed the contrary. My cooperating teacher had to reteach it, and I felt discouraged." In her fieldwork journal, Alice reflected on a similar moment:

> A lot of my students failed an assignment they did while it was just me and the sub. I feel like maybe I did not do a good enough job explaining the assignment,

but also, apparently the sub was giving students incorrect answers so I am not sure what to think.

Regardless of why Quinn's and Alice's students did not do well on their assignments, which they both linked to whether or not their teaching had been effective, it is important to note that such assessments are common sources of stress for preservice teachers (Facchinetti, 2010; Horgan et al., 2018). Furthermore, as Dunn (2018) found, high-stakes assessments that pervade classrooms are common sources of stress and burnout for many teachers that have ultimately led many to resign (p. 1).

Insufficient Content Knowledge and Pedagogical Content Knowledge

Shulman (1986) pioneered the theory that teachers must have sufficient academic content knowledge *in addition to* knowledge of how to teach students that content effectively. As Kleickmann et al. (2013) wrote of Shulman's theory:

> CK [content knowledge] represents teachers' understanding of the subject matter taught. According to Shulman (1986), "[t]he teacher need not only understand that something is so, the teacher must further understand why it is so" (p. 9). Thus, the emphasis is on a deep understanding of the subject matter taught at school. (p. 91)

The authors continued that "PCK [pedagogical content knowledge] is the knowledge needed to make subject matter accessible to students (Shulman, 1986)" (p. 91). For the preservice teachers in this study, there were entries in their fieldwork journals in which they described feeling that they lacked both the content knowledge and the pedagogical content knowledge to teach their students effectively, and that being unable to do so made them feel unsuccessful as developing teachers. For example, Selena wrote, "During tutoring I found myself doubting what I was saying. I kept questioning if what I was teaching the students was the 'right' way." Alycia had a similar experience and wrote, "I feel like I confused a student because I wasn't familiar with the material," as did Nora, who wrote, "I was teaching a student the difference between erosion and weathering, but I could not help explain it clearly." In all these instances, they felt they were unsuccessful in teaching their students because they believed they lacked the content knowledge and pedagogical content knowledge to do so effectively (Kleickmann et al., 2013; Shulman, 1986).

Leslie had a moment similar to other preservice teachers who thought they were teaching their students effectively only later to find out she had not. She also linked this to her lack of knowledge of a particular subject matter (i.e., content knowledge):

> I found out that I've apparently been learning how to do syllables all wrong. I felt frustrated because even when I looked on Google, it matched my way of

thinking, but apparently that is the wrong way. So I guess I'm still confused on how to do it now.

In all of these instances, there was a common experience of not having the content knowledge needed in the moment, or not yet having the skill to convey the content knowledge in a way that would make sense to their students (i.e., PCK). These are common experiences among experienced teachers as well (Shulman, 1986). However, these preservice teachers directly linked their perceived lack of CK and PCK in their fieldwork journals to feeling ineffective as developing teachers.

Developing Questions and Ideas for Next Time

As their teacher education program went on, the preservice teachers wrote more in their fieldwork journals about how they grappled with questions about the stressors they were experiencing while teaching their students academic content. For example, Anna wrote:

> I don't know if I should have let them pick their own groups. . . . There are benefits but some students are really struggling with the material because they lose focus working with their friend. Some groups do not have a lot on their presentation poster.

This journal entry demonstrated Anna's awareness of the different pedagogical decisions she could make when it came to choosing a particular instructional method (i.e., student- or teacher-chosen groups). Although she expressed this was a challenge, she also expressed concrete options for herself as to what to do, which may demonstrate that her pedagogical content knowledge (Shulman, 1986) was developing. Furthermore, by recognizing that she had options as a teacher, her journal entry appeared to contrast with the helplessness she and the other preservice teachers described in other journal entries.

Quinn wrote about an experience where she questioned what to do next time:

> I have a student who constantly is asking me for help even though she can do much of it already. I need to work on helping these students help themselves. So many of them need constant validation, I end up over-helping. It's frustrating because I want to help, but I need to know when to not.

Like Anna, Quinn's journal entry demonstrated that she knew her students' capabilities and was thinking about how she could best support them when it came to deciding when to help and when to let them work independently. For Quinn and Anna, realizing that there are options available for how to proceed even if they have not yet made a decision might indicate that they felt less overwhelmed by the challenges associated with teaching their students academic content. This may be connected to an increased development of their pedagogical content knowledge (Shulman, 1986), or to the fact that they have had more time in their field placements and therefore more opportunities to gain practical teaching experience, which is associated with reductions in stress and increased mastery (Horgan et al., 2018; Murray-Harvey et al., 2000; Onchwari, 2010).

For some of these preservice teachers, an apparent increase in pedagogical content knowledge and reductions in stress seemed evident as time went on in their teacher education program. For example, Nora wrote in her fieldwork journal that "[t]his semester I learned to be confident and bold while teaching. . . . I felt more successes this semester than unsuccesses [sic]." Similarly, Maria wrote about an experience where she demonstrated her increasing pedagogical content knowledge when she forgot a material she needed for a lesson and found an alternative:

> This week I felt unsuccessful when I forgot to bring a material that I needed in order to teach my lesson. My CT had asked me to bring Cookie Crisp cereal as manipulatives to teach my math lesson. However, I forgot to bring the Cookie Crisp cereal with me to class, and I saw how this immediately put stress on me to perform well during my lesson. I was able to think of an alternative manipulative that I could create by cutting out cookies that I made from paper.

In these examples, these preservice teachers saw that there may be several options available to them when things do not go as planned while teaching and that their increasing awareness of these options might make their mistakes teaching children academics feel less stressful or challenging (Horgan et al., 2018). As other researchers have found, the realization that there are alternatives may be due to an increase in pedagogical content knowledge (Shulman, 1986), an increase in practical experience (Onchwari, 2010), or perhaps some other phenomenon not yet uncovered in the extant research.

As the teacher education program continued, other preservice teachers in this study began to move beyond posing questions about what they should do the next time they felt challenged by teaching academic content to their students and provided themselves with concrete ideas of what to try the next time they encountered a similar situation. For example, Tamara wrote, "The students didn't fully grasp the concept of main idea after I taught my lesson. I needed to do more modeling and review before I asked them to do the accompanying activity." In this way, Tamara understood what went wrong while teaching this activity and had an idea (i.e., "more modeling") for what she might do next time to help her students "grasp the concept."

Amy described a similar experience: "The literature circle with my small group did not go quite as I intended, with students getting a little off track.

I will need to be more specific with what I'm expecting our time to look like." Like Tamara, Amy recognized that something got "off track" when teaching her students. While Tamara believed that more modeling and review would make teaching her students academics less challenging, Amy felt that being more specific with her expectations of her students would lead to greater success.

Similarly, Leslie wrote, "I ran out of time on my lesson. I need to work more on my time management!" Like many of the preservice teachers in this study, Leslie expressed that time management was a challenge (Horgan et al., 2018); however, like some of the other preservice teachers, she expressed that this was something she could address the next time she encountered this challenge.

Selena reflected in her journal:

> I found myself trying to make the project very structured and rigid. I kept saying things like "do it like THIS" and "see how I did this?" I think that I should make sure to go back and let the students know that they can make the project their own, as long as they have a few key points on there.

Selena encountered a common challenge preservice teachers face in her lesson—coming in with a plan, not wanting to waiver from it, but realizing afterward that teaching is complex and "multifaceted" when faced with "real" teaching situations (Onchwari, 2010).

For these preservice teachers, there was a shift in the ways they wrote about the challenges they experienced teaching academics to children over time in the teacher education program. Rather than only writing about experiences in which their teaching did not go well (as happened in the first half of their teacher education program), they began to ponder what they could do next time they encountered a similar stressful teaching challenge.

Shifting Gears in Real Time

In some instances, these preservice teachers were able to find and take the opportunity to shift gears in the moment while teaching their field students academic content to avoid the challenges that many described in their journals and self-compassionate letters. For example, Tamara wrote:

> It was time for the students to do independent work for the author study lesson and they were not on task. However, it showed me another real side of teaching—the fact that it is okay to abandon aspects of a plan when they are not going as expected. So, I had them stop working on that activity for the day and we went back to it the next day with no issues.

Here, Tamara was getting firsthand experience with "the multifaceted nature of teaching" that has caused many other preservice teachers to feel stressed (Onchwari, 2010). However, she was able to shift gears while teaching and "abandon aspects of a plan when they are not going as expected" and return to her lesson the following day with "no issues." Rather than being left feeling uncertain about the complexities of teaching that these preservice teachers described in their journals, Tamara was able to adapt in the moment.

Selena had a similar realization to Tamara when she wrote, "One of my writing lessons didn't go too well, the students were not engaged at all, and I had to make a teacher choice and scrapped the idea all together." Here, she demonstrated that she was able to identify that her lesson was not going well and successfully respond to the challenge she was experiencing in the moment by "scrapp[ing] the idea all together," which she called a "teacher choice." Borko and Cadwell (1982), who are often associated with the study of teachers' decision-making processes, found that "teachers attend to student characteristics in making these judgements" or "decisions in the realm of classroom organization and management" (p. 608). Similarly, Tamara and Selena's decisions to abandon their lessons, as they both described, were responses to demonstrated "student characteristics" (i.e., a lack of student engagement and not being on task) connected to classroom management (p. 608).

Attempting to Fix Mistakes in the Moment

Amy described a moment in her journal in which she felt she had "flubbed a lesson." She wrote, "I flubbed a lesson and did not realize until I was in the middle of it. I worked with what I had, but I definitely felt flustered." Despite feeling "flustered," Amy was able to work through her mistake. Rather than "scrapping" her lesson as Tamara and Selena did, Amy made a different decision to keep going. As Borko and Cadwell (1982) wrote, "Perhaps the most important finding to emerge from this study [of teacher decision-making] was the extent to which individual differences exist in teachers' decision policies" (p. 608). These "individual differences" also were evident in Tamara, Selena, and Amy's journals about their own decision-making processes as well, given the variability with which they described those processes, and ultimately, their "teacher choice" (Selena).

Bob also demonstrated the variability of the teacher decision-making process when she addressed a mistake she made in the moment while teaching her students academics:

> I taught something completely wrong. I was filling out a language chart with the students and accidentally mixed up topic and theme. I'd had students explain what the theme was but really, we were talking about topic and vice versa.

> Luckily, I caught my mistake and told the kids that they should've definitely called me out on my mistake! I told them in the future they should feel free to politely point out my mistakes and that it's okay 'cause I'm human and can be wrong too.

Like Tamara, Selena, and Amy, Bob recognized that something went wrong in her teaching that needed to be addressed. She demonstrated a similar strategy to Amy when she attempted to work through the challenge in the moment (unlike Tamara and Selena, who chose to stop their lessons and move on to something else). Interestingly, Bob took her mistake as an opportunity to connect with her students and allow them to teach her, which again demonstrates the variability in approaches teachers make in their decision-making processes (Borko & Cadwell, 1982).

Experimenting With Solutions and Increasing Clarity About Challenges

As time in their teacher education program continued to pass, these preservice teachers continued to experiment with solutions in real time more and more when it came to teaching academic content to their students. For example, Nicole wrote:

> I think I feel unsuccessful when I am trying to explain a concept that my student is struggling with grasping. I think teaching my Math lesson some were able to catch on really easily and be able to explain to their classmates what they did. While others felt confused with the steps or the process. I did work with them one on one and told them to do each step at a time and then they were able to grasp it. I am working on letting kids share that don't usually get to be called on. I know there are some kids who always raise their hand, but I need to think about who I call on usually and try and switch that around.

While Nicole described this as a moment in which she felt unsuccessful teaching academics, she also had some successes with how she experimented with solutions in real time (i.e., working one on one with students until they understood), which may indicate her developing her pedagogical content knowledge in real time (Shulman, 1986).

Similarly, in Elaine's fieldwork journal from the third and final semester of the teacher education program, she reflected on how time management was a specific challenge she wanted to work on when it came to teaching academic content to her students, which, as noted throughout this book, is a common stressor for preservice teachers (Facchinetti, 2010; Horgan et al., 2018). She wrote:

> I wish I had spent more time wrapping up the . . . project and making sure students got what they were supposed to from it. I think having students check

each other's work might've helped or even simply asking students what was hard or what was easy or what were some things they noticed. That would've solidified what they already knew and were working towards the entire time.

Here, Elaine expressed that more time would have been useful in "wrapping up" a project she was working on with her students and would have allowed them to "solidif[y] what they . . . knew." As is the case for many preservice teachers, her "crowded curriculum" (Facchinetti, 2010, in Horgan et al., 2018 pp. 217–218) in which it was necessary to move on from one topic to the next was stressful. However, Elaine took the opportunity to reflect on—and offer specific ideas about—what she could do to feel more successful teaching her students academic content the next time she experienced a similar challenge (i.e., soliciting feedback from students).

Wanting to Veer From Their Cooperating Teachers' Lesson Plans

Elaine, Leslie, and Quinn described moments in their semester 3 fieldwork journals that demonstrated a desire to shift away from their cooperating teachers' plans either to make it feel like the lesson was their own or because the current plan was confusing to them or their students. Elaine wrote:

> I don't know that I felt as unsuccessful as I do nervous. I'm doing a Total Teach in Science with [my cooperating teacher] and I'm trying to lesson plan using the materials he gave me and it's kind of nerve-racking and annoying. I want to make it my own but it's hard. I also want to make sure I'm hitting the [content standards] and making it engaging and all of these things. There's just a lot going through my head about lesson planning.

Here, Elaine showed that she wanted more autonomy in her decision-making when teaching her students (Borko & Cadwell, 1982) and that not being able to make her science lesson her own was "nerve-racking and annoying."

For Elaine, who wrote here about her "total teach" experience (during which these preservice teachers were in charge of all aspects of planning and teaching for at least 2 weeks in their final semester in this teacher education program), new challenges with understanding her role in her cooperating teacher's classroom (Horgan et al., 2018; Zimmerman et al., 2008) emerged. Although this was meant to be Elaine's time to be the teacher in her cooperating teacher's classroom, she felt her cooperating teacher would not give her the space to make these decisions independently.

Leslie described a similar experience of feeling that she had to use her cooperating teacher's plans when she wrote, "I taught text features. I was not able to make my own lesson, so I had to go along with my CT's plans. The whole lesson was pretty confusing." Leslie believed if she had been able to make her own lesson, it would not have been "confusing," and she would have felt more successful teaching her students about text features.

In a similar vein, Quinn wrote:

> I almost gave one student the wrong accommodations for his IEP [individualized education plan] and my CT snapped at me about it. I was not modifying the material, just trying to find ways to help him complete his work faster while still completing the same content. Even if it is not in his IEP, I didn't really see the harm in it. Isn't that RTI [response to intervention]?

Although Quinn may not have fully realized the legal implications of not following a student's IEP—one of the "multifaceted" complexities of teaching (Onchwari, 2010, p. 392)—she felt that her approach to supporting this particular student would have been more effective than what her cooperating teacher was obligated to do given this student's IEP. Quinn's plan may very well have been more effective than what was written in her student's IEP, but she did not get the opportunity to find out.

ADDRESSING THE STRESS OF DELIVERING ACADEMIC CONTENT TO STUDENTS WITH SELF-COMPASSION

Many of the self-compassionate letters written by the preservice teachers in this study focused on addressing the challenges they experienced when they didn't feel confident delivering academic content to their field students. As you read in the previous section, feeling unsuccessful when teaching academic content was a common experience among these preservice teachers at every stage of the teacher education program in which they were enrolled. What follows are excerpts from the self-compassionate letters these preservice teachers wrote themselves in response to the challenge of teaching academic content to children. All of them contain specific phrases that are emblematic of the three components of self-compassion: mindfulness, self-kindness, and common humanity (Neff, 2003). I hope that you may be inspired by their words when writing your own self-compassionate letter at the end of this chapter.

Excerpts From Educators' Self-Compassionate Letters

It was inspiring to read the way these preservice teachers demonstrated self-compassion when responding to an experience or perceived flaw about themselves as developing teachers when it came to teaching academic content to children. For example, Amy wrote:

> I really helped him and working with him was so great. I need to recognize, though, that I did not yet have the experience (and know-how) in the classroom to assert

myself. Had I known how, I would have made sure I made time for my other students. It is okay that you didn't though. You did your best in the situation you were given, and now you know for next time. Make sure to be assertive next semester! You got this!

By writing that she "did not yet have the experience" and "[i]t is okay that [she] did not know," Amy acknowledged that not having that experience or know-how in the past would not limit her capacity to gain that experience and know-how in the present or in future teaching situations. As Pintrich and Blumenfeld (1985, in Johnston, 2003) wrote, "when a child tries something and does not succeed, we need to turn that event toward a narrative and identity that will be useful for the future. If children are not making errors, they are not putting themselves in learning situations" (Kindle location 878–887). While Pintrich and Blumenfeld (1985) and Johnston (2003) were referring specifically to the importance of errors in children's learning processes, Amy, perhaps unknowingly, applied this concept to herself. Meaning, she acknowledged that not having the "know-how," or pedagogical content knowledge (Shulman, 1986), did not mean she would never have the "know-how" as a developing teacher.

Maria wrote that "'failure' is a very useful tool that you can learn from" in one of her self-compassionate letters from early on in the teacher education program:

Dear friend, <3

I think that is great that you tried to jump into a lesson! You could have expressed to your CT that you would have liked to have been given at least a few mins notice ahead of time, but I think that fact that you took on the challenge can be thought of as one of your successes. As a teacher you will need that confidence to jump into action and accept that "failure" is a very useful tool that you can learn from. Maybe the kids were not as engaged as you would like and you felt awkward in front of the whole class, but remember that you were also unaware that you would be doing this today. I think it's good to remember to enjoy teaching. Enjoy that present moment when you're with the kids! Make eye-contact! make jokes! And don't be afraid to put your own spin on things—what works for your CT will be different from what feels genuine to you and that's ok too :)

-Have fun
~Love,
Imaginary Friend <3

Just as a teacher "can limit this possibility [that a child will avoid making mistakes] by overtly valuing children's exploration of new tactics and possibilities," Maria demonstrated in her letter that she valued her attempts at trying "new tactics and possibilities"—even though she did not yet feel prepared for it (Pintrich & Blumenfeld, 1985, in Johnston, 2003, Kindle location 878–887). In this way, she was able to reframe this moment in which she felt unsuccessful as a successful one. As with the other preservice teachers in the study guiding this book, Maria's self-compassionate letter is imbued with self-compassionate language that is encouraging and self-kind, rather than critical and judgmental (Neff, 2011; Neff & Germer, 2018).

Elaine wrote a self-compassionate letter about a similar experience to Maria's and Amy's in which she acknowledged that she had made a mistake but did not want to define herself by that mistake:

Dear Elaine,

You are so much more than your one mistake. don't let that hinder you + don't judge yourself based on it. There are so many things that you do that amaze me. Your passion for teaching children + making an impact on their lives is one I wish to encompass. You make decisions every day that are positive + that make you a better teacher + person. Remember those moments. Remember all the good that you've done + all the good that you will continue to do. Everyone makes mistakes, even veteran teachers. What makes you a great educator is that you take that mistake + you learn from it. Next time you won't grab him you'll appeal to his love of flowers. No matter the mistakes you make children will still love + adore you. That's what makes them great.

-Your imaginary friend! <3

Elaine demonstrated self-compassion (common humanity specifically) when she reminded herself that "[e]veryone makes mistakes, even veteran teachers." Like Maria and Amy, Elaine encouraged herself not to define herself by this one mistake because of all the other "things that [she does] that amaze" her. She showed in her letter that she believed that when people "are not making errors, they are not putting themselves in learning situations" (Pintrich & Blumenfeld 1985, in Johnston, 2003, Kindle location 878–887) in ways similar to Maria and Amy.

It appeared that one way many of these preservice teachers emphasized mindfulness in their self-compassionate letters was to acknowledge that a particular stressor, challenge, or feeling of inadequacy was normal because they did not yet have the teaching experience they needed to respond successfully during particular challenging moments. In this way, they acknowledged in their letters why a certain experience in their field placements may have happened a certain way without judging themselves for the outcomes; to remove the judgment from the outcome of an experience is an act of mindfulness (Bishop et al., 2004; Kabat-Zinn, 1994; Neff & Germer, 2018; Siegel, 2010). For example, Amy wrote:

> This week, I finished up my literature unit + it felt so sloppy. I did not feel that I drove home the importance of the themes. The students were also being very silly towards the end. But that is okay. I had never had to wrap up a lit unit before, so it is only natural that I would stumble somewhere. Now is the time for me to make mistakes. And even as a teacher, not every lesson is going to go flawlessly. It will be more productive to think "what can I do differently next time" instead of dwelling on what didn't go well. As always, you've got this! Just power through and do your best.

Amy recognized that dwelling on what went wrong would not be particularly helpful to her as a developing teacher when she encouraged herself to see experiences of failure as learning opportunities rather than flaws within herself (Bishop et al., 2004; Kabat-Zinn, 1994; Neff & Germer, 2018; Siegel, 2010).

In one of her self-compassionate letters, Quinn wrote about feeling "unprepared" and "pretty terrible" about an experience teaching her students:

> Quinn,
>
> When you were unprepared and not feeling yourself the other day, it felt pretty terrible. It's impossible to always be your best self when teaching. Sometimes, the stars just don't align, and because of various reasons, we perform in a way that doesn't please us. Please remember that this happens to even the most seasoned teachers, and that it's going to happen to you. Be easy on yourself. Everybody has those days.

Here, Quinn demonstrated a sense of common humanity in her letter by connecting to others (Neff, 2011), who, in the case of this letter, were "seasoned teachers." As Neff and Germer (2018) wrote of common humanity, many people—teachers included—"fall into the trap of believing that things are 'supposed' to go well and that something has gone wrong when they don't.... [However] we'll make mistakes and experience hardships on a regular basis" (pp. 10–11). By acknowledging in this letter that even the most experienced teachers have their lessons not go as planned, Quinn demonstrated this particular aspect of common humanity. In all of these examples, these preservice teachers showed in their self-compassionate letters that their mistakes were opportunities to continue to learn more about teaching academic content to children.

In one of Anna's self-compassionate letters, she wrote:

> You are still learning to be an effective teacher. In fact, you will always be learning. Perfection is not going to happen, so breathe and know that your best is good enough. You made a mistake, it is okay. Mistakes let you reflect and you will catch yourself next time if a similar opportunity arises. Don't forget about looking at the positive experiences that have happened. This. is. your. year.

Here, like Quinn, Anna reminded herself that mistakes are opportunities to "reflect" and improve as a teacher. Additionally, she encouraged herself to look "at the positive experiences" she had in her field placement. Rather than be consumed by her "mistake," Anna "put a supportive arm around [her] own shoulder" (Neff & Germer, 2018, p. 10) and pointed out the positive side of these stressful experiences in the teacher education program.

Sally also expressed in her self-compassionate letters that there were positive aspects to the challenges related to teaching academic content to her field students. In one of these letters, she wrote:

My Sweet S,

Don't doubt your presence in the classroom. I know at times you feel inadequate, unprepared, and just plain stressed out. But know that you are appreciated, by both the teachers and students. You are smart, with great ideas for your own classroom. You will be an amazing teacher one day. Just remember that you are learning so much and to just embrace the time that you have left. Be present + be happy. Love yourself always.

xoxo Sally

Like Anna, Sally mindfully acknowledged her feelings of inadequacy and stress (Bishop et al., 2004; Kabat-Zinn, 1994; Neff & Germer, 2018; Siegel, 2010) but did not define herself by these feelings. Instead, she wrote to herself like a friend by reminding herself how "appreciated" she is by teachers and students and that she is "learning so much" as she works to develop into "an amazing teacher" (Johnston, 2003; Neff, 2003, 2011; Neff & Germer, 2018).

As her time in the teacher education program went on, Sally wrote another self-compassionate letter in which she identified the positive side of going through the stressors of learning to be a teacher:

My dearest Sally,

You are almost done with your second semester of placement! You will be student teaching in just a few short months and you will crush it! You have already gained a lot of knowledge over the past year. You've learned, now all you need to do is put a foot forward, breathe, and teach. You have people to support you. Don't stress. Just enjoy this time—learn more, fail, grow, adapt. This process was made for you to learn, you don't have to be the perfect teacher to be a great teacher.
Enjoy this season,

<3 Sally

Here, Sally actually encouraged herself to "fail" and framed failure as part of the "process . . . for [her] to learn" how to become a teacher, not something to "stress" about. In other words, she expressed that failure was necessary to her development as a teacher, just as Johnston posited that failure and mistakes were critical to students' learning and development (2003). She also demonstrated self-compassion when she told herself "you don't have to be the perfect teacher to be a great teacher." Additionally, she showed that she cared deeply for herself in this letter (e.g., <3 sign, "my dearest Sally") just as she was, "with all [her] very human imperfections" (Neff, 2011, p. 16).

Leslie, like Anna and Sally, also wrote self-compassionate letters that encouraged her to view her experiences with challenges as learning experiences that were making her a better teacher. In one such letter, Leslie wrote:

> I just want to remind you that you are doing an amazing job. Remember that this is a process + not everything is going to be perfect. You are growing as a person and as a teacher! Try not to be hard on yourself when your lessons don't go as planned because you will get better. You are wonderful, Leslie!
>
> Love,
> Leslie

Like Sally, Leslie acknowledged that perfection does not exist (Neff & Germer, 2018) and that her time in the teacher education program was a "process" that supported her "grow[th] as a person and as a teacher." In another letter, Leslie reflected self-compassionately on an experience in which she ran out of time teaching a lesson and found a positive side to this challenging experience:

> Dear Leslie,
>
> I know you ran out of time in your lesson this week but it's okay! It was your first official big lesson + you did amazing! You were very flexible with your time + gave the students more time to read, which was a good move. This is all part of the process + it's better to not speed through a lesson [because] then they won't learn anything. You are growing so much through this process. Keep up the good work. You're going to be a spectacular teacher.

Time is a common source of stress for preservice teachers (Horgan et al., 2018; Zimmerman et al., 2008). Leslie, however, was able to find some positives in this stressful moment in her field placement: Her students had "more time to read" and if she were to "speed through a lesson . . . they [wouldn't have] learn[ed] anything." Here, her ability to recognize what she could do to maximize her students' learning opportunities when she was running out of time demonstrated a perceived feeling of success with her teacher decision-making process (Borko & Cadwell, 1982) and her pedagogical content knowledge (Shulman, 1986). Finally, despite running out of time, Leslie still felt that she would become "a spectacular teacher."

Quinn acknowledged that learning to be a teacher was a process:

> Quinn,
>
> Whenever my social studies lesson didn't go how you wanted it, you got pretty upset at yourself. But it is important to think of teaching as an experiment, and when something isn't working, we get to change it! You get so much valuable information from your mistakes! It's ok to feel disappointed, but be gentle with yourself.

Like the other preservice teachers' letters that found positive aspects to the mistakes they made when teaching academic content to their field students, Quinn wrote that she believed she could "get so much valuable information from [her] mistakes" to adjust her teaching in the future. Even though her lesson did not go as planned, she acted as her own friend by comforting herself (Neff, 2003, 2011; Neff & Germer, 2018).

Amy also had an experience where her lesson did not go as planned, offered herself self-compassion, and found positives:

> I felt unsuccessful when first working with a small group of my special ed students. I had not yet done this before with more than two students. On that day I worked with 5 of them. I recognize that I was not yet equipped to do this and see why I struggled to work with them. I had a difficult time managing behavior and getting many of them to focus on the assignment. But that is okay. I know that things do not always go perfectly on the first time and that is just fine! It didn't stop me from trying again, this time with a bit of scaffolding support from the SPED [special education] teacher. After trying again, I did just fine, so that first rocky time is nothing to worry about because I got this. Those areas that you don't feel good at yet are just things you need to practice + you'll get better at it. :)

In addition to soothing herself after a challenging experience (Neff, 2003, 2011; Neff & Germer, 2018), she, like the other preservice teachers, found positives. For Amy, "trying again" and doing "just fine" showed her that teaching requires "practice" in order to "get better at it." Here, she recognized in her self-compassionate letter what research shows, which is that the most experienced teachers (i.e., those with the most "practice") are the most effective teachers (e.g., Fantilli & McDougall, 2009).

Preparing to Write Your Own Self-Compassionate Letter That Addresses the Stress of Delivering Academic Content to Students

The examples from these preservice teachers' self-compassionate letters demonstrated all the components of self-compassion (mindfulness, self-kindness, and common humanity [Neff, 2003, 2011; Neff & Germer, 2018]) while also demonstrating that they could address the challenges they were experiencing and the mistakes they made teaching academic content in their field placements—namely, that these mistakes and challenges were not going to prevent them from becoming good teachers. In fact, it seemed that they began to recognize that making mistakes was both inevitable and necessary in what some described as "the process" of becoming a teacher.

With all of this in mind, I ask that you complete the following exercise, which will lead to you writing your first self-compassionate letter related to the challenge of teaching academic content to your students.

> This activity is based on Neff's (2011) "exploring self-compassion through letter-writing" (pp. 16–17) prompt. In Neff's (2011) original prompt, she encouraged the person completing it to consider what this unconditionally loving friend would say to them about their perceived flaw, challenge, or mistake (pp. 16–17). I have learned from the preservice teachers I worked with on my dissertation study that it appears to be easier for developing teachers to reverse this and instead imagine what *they* would say to their friend about their mistake or flaw instead of what this friend would say to them (Barry, 2021). I don't have data to support this, but my hunch is that it may be easier and perhaps more comfortable to imagine giving out love and support in the form of self-compassionate affirmations than it is to imagine receiving it; at least at first.

1. Think about a mistake you made when delivering academic content to your students recently. When you think about this mistake, what words and phrases come to mind about your abilities as a teacher or your "worth" as a person? Are there parts of your identity that you feel may elicit prejudice in others about your abilities as a teacher? Write down these words or phrases that come to mind.
2. Consider this question: Do you have a classmate or colleague that you feel close to, either in your teacher education program or at your school? If yes, I want you to picture that person right now. If you don't have someone like that, it's ok; instead, imagine someone else in your life that you feel close to or imagine someone that you could feel close to.
3. I want you to imagine that this friend or colleague—real or imaginary—has confided in you that they have made the *exact* same mistake when teaching academic content to their students. The conditions were identical, as was the mistake that they made. The only difference is that it was *they* who made the mistake instead of you. What words or phrases come to mind that you would say to this friend or colleague about the mistake that they

made? Just as you did earlier, write down the words or phrases that come to mind.
4. Now, compare what you've written down for points 1 and 3 (above). Are there differences between what you wrote when *you* were the teacher making the mistake versus when this friend or colleague was the teacher making the mistake, even though the conditions were identical? Well, if there is a difference, know that you aren't alone; most people are much more critical of themselves than they are about the people they care about. With time and practice, you can reframe the stressors and challenges you are experiencing as a developing teacher to be less self-critical and more like how you would respond to that friend or colleague (Barry, 2021, 2022, 2023; Neff & Germer, 2018;). This is self-compassion, and just like learning to teach effectively, developing self-compassion is a skill that takes time and practice.

Write Your Own Self-Compassionate Letter That Addresses the Stress of Delivering Academic Content to Students

Now, take some time to write your letter. At first, I want you to picture that friend or colleague in your teacher education program (real or imagined) you feel close to that you were just thinking about in the previous section. Imagine again that *they made the exact same mistake that you did* and that the conditions were exactly the same. Look back at what you wrote about *what you would say to them* if they confided in you that they had made that same mistake. Begin writing a letter to convey what you would tell them. However, instead of addressing the letter to the real or imagined friend, address the letter to yourself.

Be sure to include how you would convey to yourself that *mistakes are part of learning to become a teacher* and that *these mistakes don't define your worth as a person.* Will you connect with yourself about mistakes you made while learning to become a teacher or remind yourself about other common mistakes that developing teachers make? If you feel there are parts of your identity that may prejudice others against your ability to be an effective teacher, how do you encourage yourself to not buy into that stereotype?

Finally, given that making more mistakes while teaching is inevitable, how would you encourage yourself to be kinder to yourself in the future when you make a mistake like this?

The final part of the practice is to "put [the letter] . . . down for a little while. Then come back and read it again, really letting the words sink in. Feel the compassion as it pours into you, soothing and comforting you like a cool breeze on a hot day" (Neff, 2011, p. 17).

If you're feeling stuck, read the self-compassionate letter I wrote to myself about bombing my lesson about making an "animals that hibernate counting book" with my pre-K students when I was student teaching (see opening vignette).

Example: My Self-Compassionate Letter About My Hibernation Lesson

As promised, I've included my response to the challenge I shared at the beginning of this chapter when trying to teach my pre-K field students about animals that hibernate. I hope my response to the prompt helps you conceptualize how you might write yours.

> Dear Dave,
>
> Even though it's been 16 years since you prepared and taught this lesson on animals that hibernate, I can still remember how much time, effort, and thought you put into it and how crushed you were that it didn't go as planned. It must have been so frustrating to have spent all that time making the collages of each animal's hibernation environment, scanning them, and printing them, to have the kids rush through it and not really get it. You even put all that time into drawing cute little hibernating animals for them to count and glue to each page so they could have their own counting book! What I want you to remember is that even the best plans and the most well-thought-out activities don't always go well. I also know that being the only male student in the program makes you feel you need to disprove the stereotypes about male early childhood teachers of being lazy, disorganized, and ineffective compared to female teachers, and it's exhausting always feeling like you need to do more than everyone else. I know it also makes you feel that expressing frustration with students—even in a kind way—will be perceived as mean or anger. Rather than feel stymied by how hard it was to get through this with your AM pre-K students, let's take a look at what went well.
>
> First, how awesome is it that a student was so excited about the project you were doing with her classmates that she kept coming over to check in with you about when she'd get to do it? I know you felt snappy with her because it was hard to take your attention off the students you were working with—that must have been really hard to be managing so many students all at once. Because you were monitoring what they were doing so closely, you weren't able to give this other student your attention. If you were to do this again, maybe you could tell her that you were going to set a timer for when it would be her turn, and that you'd come get her when the timer went off.
>
> Second, you were so fortunate to be able to have a second chance with this project with the PM group! You realized that 5 students were too many so you reduced the number to 4, and instead of giving them all the pages at once, you just gave them one at a time. That seemed to really help keep them focused and on track, which is wonderful. This means that you learned from your mistake and made changes to improve your teaching—in the very same day! That is wonderful and you should be proud of how quickly you were able to shift gears to make your lesson work. Finally, you were able to detect when one of your groups of pre-K students was losing interest

in the project and chose not to take it personally—you just ensured that they got the concept of where certain animals hibernate and matching the page number with the number of hibernating animals they were supposed to glue on each page a few times, and then moved on. Knowing when to stop and move on is such an important skill for teachers to have—think of how much worse it would've been if you made them stay when they were feeling done!

Even though this was a hard day, you learned a lot about yourself as a teacher and grew a lot in a single day. I am proud of you and I hope you're feeling proud of yourself!

Love,
Dave

I hope that you see this practice of addressing the stressors you are likely experiencing in delivering academic content to your students with self-compassion is something that you can do any time you need to; this exercise should not be seen as a "one and done" activity. As many of the preservice teachers described in Chapter 2 of this book, with time, this practice of writing self-compassionate letters became how they spoke to themselves when these inevitable challenges arose as new and developing teachers. Further, the act of writing these letters several times ($n=11$) over their 3-semester teacher education program significantly increased their self-compassion scores (Barry, 2021, 2022, 2023), which, as other researchers have demonstrated, is highly correlated with higher levels of job satisfaction and fewer instances of burnout among professional caregivers (Barnard & Curry, 2012; Shapiro et al., 2005). Given all you do to support your young students, I know that you, too, are a professional caregiver, and it is my sincerest hope that you may experience similar benefits.

CHAPTER 4

The Stress of Meeting Students' Social, Emotional, and Behavioral Needs

> My First Day of School—Fall 2007
>
> The big day arrived. My classroom was finally organized and set up in a way that reflected my impression of what a kindergarten classroom should look like. My teaching assistant had been a dream in helping me get organized in those few days leading up to the start of the school year, particularly with the administrative tasks of figuring out how our students would get to and from school every day. Some students would be dropped off and picked up by family members, others were enrolled in before- and after-school programs, others would take the bus, and still others would come and go in any combination of these ways depending on the day of the week.
>
> I still had no idea what I was doing when it came to teaching, but one thing I *had* learned in student teaching was how to connect with children. I decided that that would really be the focus those first couple weeks of school—especially on the first day, when we would just be learning routines (and I do mean we—the children *and* I needed to learn those routines). I was amazed that within the first hour I already knew all the children's names, and by the end of the day, I had an opportunity to talk with each of them about all sorts of things: favorite colors, books, snacks, TV shows, things to do on the playground, and so on. Well, almost everyone.
>
> I had a really hard time making a connection with one of my students on that first day of school—we'll call him Scott. He didn't talk to me or my assistant. He didn't really seem to know how to play with or near other children yet, and he was visibly angry about being at school. The only time he'd uncross his arms was to knock over another student's block structure or to mime fighting moves if anyone came close. I did what I had always done as a student teacher and told him that "we don't do fighting moves in kindergarten" and "we don't knock down what our friends are building"; he just looked at me and scrunched his eyebrows and crossed his arms. It was just the first day, and I told myself that "we'd" get there eventually.
>
> The end of the day came quickly, and I felt relieved that I had my first day under my belt as my assistant and I brought our students to their various end-of-day destinations. As I was saying goodbye to the last student I was dismissing to their family, my assistant

came by to tell me all the children taking the bus or going to an after-school program were where they needed to be. We had made it through the first day!

We went back to our classroom to clean up and get organized for the next day. I learned that day that learning to clean up was something I would have to teach my students to do, so I was restacking blocks, putting caps on markers, and picking up snipped pieces of construction paper from the floor. About 30 minutes or so later, the principal ran into my classroom. "Where is Scott?!" she said in a panic. My assistant told her that she'd brought him to the area where he'd wait for his bus with the other children. The principal anxiously replied, "His mother was waiting for him at the bus stop, and all the other children who get off at that bus stop did, but he didn't. We don't know where he is."

I don't think I've ever been more scared in my life. It was my first day of teaching ever, and I'd experienced every teacher's worst fear: I'd lost a student.

The three of us went outside the building and started looking for him but had no idea where to even begin. This was Boston. There was a busy train station right across the street from school, and it had already been half an hour; he could be anywhere at this point. A million "what ifs?" were swirling in my head.

After a few minutes of looking that felt like an eternity, my cell phone rang. It was the principal. Scott was in the school office, reunited with his mother.

You're probably reading this and thinking he'd been in the office the whole time. It's certainly what I was thinking as I walked back into the building. It wasn't until I saw the police officer who was standing in the office that I realized that this was more than just a student hiding in the office.

I sat down with Scott, his mom, the principal, my assistant, and the police officer at the table in the office. Scott's mom was still very shaken up, understandably so, and I couldn't stop apologizing. I noticed there was another child and his mother at the table, too, but I didn't recognize them. You'll remember that Scott didn't talk to me, my assistant, or the other children that day. Thankfully, this little guy, a pre-K student, was extraordinarily verbal and had a police officer to help corroborate his story.

Apparently, when all the children in the school were being brought to the waiting areas for their various buses at the end of the day, Scott took this particular pre-K student by the hand and brought him to a *different* bus line. Not only did the two of them get in the wrong bus line, but they followed that line right onto the wrong bus and got off at the first stop, which—you got it—was not their correct bus stop. Fortunately, the parents who were meeting their own children at the bus stop noticed that no one was there to meet Scott and his pre-K buddy. Unfortunately, the bus had already left. A police officer happened to be passing by, and the group of parents flagged him down, and Scott and his new friend were brought back to school by the police officer.

I was relieved both the students were safe but certain I was going to be fired. I wasn't, as everyone but me agreed that this wasn't my fault—just a really unfortunate mistake that fortunately ended up okay.

MY OWN CHALLENGES MEETING STUDENTS' SOCIAL, EMOTIONAL, AND BEHAVIORAL NEEDS

First, I want to remind you that a situation like the one above is *highly unlikely* for others to experience during their first day of teaching. It is hard to imagine a worse first-day of being a "real" teacher (i.e., my first teaching job after graduating from college). Although I had plenty of examples from my student teaching journal about my feelings of inadequacy around supporting children's behavior and emotional needs, nothing sticks out quite like losing a student on my first day of being a "real" teacher.

The only skill I felt confident about when I started teaching was my ability to connect with children quickly and to make them feel cared for and welcome. I learned from many experiences during student teaching that supporting my students' social, emotional, and behavioral needs was the foundation that all academic learning would then build on. Despite the confidence I had that I could make these connections with my students, Scott was the exception that first day of school. While most of the children appeared to be happy and comfortable in my care, nothing I tried worked with him. Although with time he started to trust me, I never learned why he got on the wrong bus, nor why he'd brought the pre-K student with him.

WHY IS MEETING STUDENTS' SOCIAL, EMOTIONAL, AND BEHAVIORAL NEEDS STRESSFUL FOR PRESERVICE TEACHERS?

Many of the preservice early childhood teachers in my study expressed challenges with managing student behavior and complex social and emotional needs, which is common among preservice teachers (Chaplain, 2008; Horgan et al., 2018). For example, in Nora's fieldwork journal, she described an experience when:

> A student was not listening to me when I told her to sit out on the side for being disruptive. I had to tell her multiple times, but she did not get up. [My cooperating teacher] had to stand up and get her to move.

Like Nora, Elaine wrote:

> One of the students who is starting to be a little difficult told me no. I was a little shook and didn't know how to respond. At that point, my CT [cooperating teacher] told [him] that that's not acceptable and got him to do what I told him to. I also felt unsuccessful when this same student cried because I took his block center privileges away because he was being mean towards another student. I wondered if I was going too far because a student never cried from my CT taking their privileges away. She [my CT] made me feel better after explaining why

> I took them away and told me that that was the right thing to do because we don't want to reinforce his behavior. She ended up talking to him about it and sat him out for recess because he's been having some problems in other areas.

In this moment, Elaine's experience of not feeling successful while addressing her student telling her "no" and needing her cooperating teacher's support was compounded when she felt she went "too far" by taking the student's "privileges away." For Elaine and Nora, having an experienced cooperating teacher who could be supportive in these moments was helpful in addressing the behavior problem (Murray-Harvey et al., 2000), but feeling incapable of addressing these behaviors on their own appeared to make both Elaine and Nora feel unsuccessful. In a similar vein, Anna wrote:

> Henry had a breakdown. He ran away from class after having a tantrum in the classroom. I tried to get him to calm down or to distract him with sitting for a read aloud, but nothing worked. This made me feel unsuccessful because I could not defuse the situation.

In this situation, Anna felt unsuccessful because the tools at her disposal for supporting her student during his "tantrum" were ineffective.

Bob shared a common experience teachers face when she felt challenged, stressed, and "hurt" by student behavior (Chaplain, 2008; Horgan et al., 2018):

> I had asked some students to stop making fart sounds with their mouths while the substitute was speaking to the class. I was in shock because I had never seen the students lose control like that and I think I'd gone over to their group table to speak to them at least 10 or more times. My voice was basically gone by the end of the day. I had asked them to be respectful and that making tooting sounds with their mouths was extremely not okay. The substitute was an older gentleman and hard of hearing. He didn't hear the sounds and I think that made it worse because they knew he couldn't hear. I ended up having to pull the student who was the most distracting and talking with him. I asked him to come and speak with me and he said no and hid under his table. I gave him a choice saying, "You can come over here yourself and speak with me or I can come over to you. Either way, we are having a talk." I eventually got him over to where I was and I looked him in the eyes and asked him what was up. I did not raise my voice but I made sure that my voice was firm. I was shaking, and I'm pretty sure my face was red. I was just so sad and hurt and I don't know why. I wasn't angry, I was just hurt. I told him that if he kept making tooting sounds and yelling "fart" as the answer to the questions the substitute asked, I would have to write [my cooperating teacher] a letter about his behavior. I told him that I really did not want to write the letter and that I know he [could] do better in controlling his energy. I told him that I believed in him and I gave him

a high-five. I tried my best to sincerely show him that I cared about helping him. I don't know if he cared at all. I don't know if he was more respectful towards the sub when I left. I don't know if anything I said meant anything to him. I've never felt so sad, upset, defeated, and disappointed. I felt like I didn't want to be a teacher. I hate that I have to tell [my cooperating teacher] that her students were behaving this way.

Bob's description of her experience trying to manage disruptive student behavior is similar to challenges described in previous research aimed at understanding preservice teachers' stress (Chaplain, 2008; Horgan et al., 2018). However, her negative experiences with student behavior made her question whether or not she wanted to be a teacher at all. This tension illuminates what previous researchers have found regarding the ways in which teachers' methods of managing stress—whether positive or negative—can begin in their preservice teacher education programs (Gold, 1985; Horgan et al., 2018).

Similar challenges seemed evident in Tamara's fieldwork journal:

The students were doing a writing/reading activity and I could not get them to stay on level zero. I tried using a number of different strategies and management methods that [my cooperating teacher] uses, but the students refused to remain quiet.

For Tamara, though she seemed to gain confidence in attempting to use her cooperating teacher's behavior management strategies, she did not seem to feel effective in these attempts at getting her students to "remain quiet."

Although Bob and Tamara wrote of moments in which they were confronted by overt behavior challenges (e.g., laughing at or ignoring their attempts at behavior management), Sophia wrote of an experience in which she felt uncertain in how to support a student who seemed to withdraw: "I was not able to reach a student when they started acting out. He closed himself off and I felt like I couldn't push too hard." While she chose to not "push too hard" in this situation, another preservice teacher, Cara, found herself at the other end of this extreme when choosing what action to take when addressing student behavior.

In Cara's fieldwork journal, she wrote, "I literally snatched a piece of paper out of a student's hands because it was something they shouldn't have been looking at. A student told me that I was being too aggressive and should have asked nicely." As stated previously, challenges with behavior management (i.e., addressing student behavior) are common experiences among preservice teachers (Chaplain, 2008; Horgan et al., 2018), and that appeared to be the case for these preservice teachers. This seemed particularly evident given the very different ways they attempted to address student behaviors as they arose. For example, Cara chose a "fight" approach to her challenge with student behavior when she "snatched" a paper from a student's hands, while

Bob chose a "flight" approach when she walked away from the students who were laughing at her attempts to address their behavior. This is not to say that these are the same as the body's "fight or flight" response (Cannon, 1932); rather, this metaphor highlights how these two preservice teachers chose to approach challenging student behaviors with seemingly opposed methods (Borko & Cadwell, 1982). These different responses align with the "shock" Onchwari (2010) found that many preservice teachers experience when they "have broad theoretical knowledge but are challenged when faced with real situations" and are confronted with the need to "tak[e] care of children's emotional needs" when responding to their behavior (p. 392).

Linking Challenging Behavior with Role Conflict

There were several moments these preservice teachers wrote about challenging student behavior being connected to their students not "seeing" them as a teacher. The examples I share next include a direct link each preservice teacher made between a particular student's or students' behavior and their belief that this behavior was the result of the student(s) not seeing them as a "real" teacher or authority figure. This connects to the notion of role conflict that Zimmerman et al. (2008) found in their study of preservice teachers' experiences with stress; however, the conflict in understanding the role of the preservice teacher in these instances was not felt or expressed by the preservice teacher. Rather, the conflict about that role was demonstrated by how their *field students* responded to them. What follows are examples from the preservice teachers' fieldwork journals that describe similar experiences with challenging behaviors that they believed resulted from their students not seeing them as a teacher (Chaplain, 2008; Horgan et al., 2018; Zimmerman et al., 2008). Alice described such an experience:

> I had a student throwing water at other students as they washed their hands. I asked him calmly to stop 2 or 3 times. He completely ignored me and kept throwing the water. I took his arm and brought him in front of me and asked him "Did you hear me ask you to stop?" He stared at me blankly. I became very frustrated. He then started mocking me saying "Did you hear me [ask you to] stop." I do not feel respected by some of the children.

For Alice, not feeling "respected" and being "mocked" by her students were stressful moments that she felt meant that her students did not see her as a teacher (Chaplain, 2008; Horgan et al., 2018; Zimmerman et al., 2008).

Anna had a similar experience that she wrote about in her fieldwork journal:

> One of the students did not listen to me and kept doing what he wanted. He would respond with either "Why?" or "No." This made me feel unsuccessful because after

all this time, some students did not see me as an authority figure and felt that it was okay to talk back when all I was doing was giving advice or trying to redirect them.

Anna expressed frustration that her students did not yet see her as "an authority figure" (i.e., a teacher) even though she had been a part of their classroom for nearly a semester (Chaplain, 2008; Horgan et al., 2018; Zimmerman et al., 2008). Leslie described a similar frustrating experience when she wrote, "I could not get one of my students to do an assignment. It was a little frustrating because I felt like he was not taking me seriously." Leslie, Alice, and Anna believed that students demonstrate that they "see" someone as a teacher when they follow directions, redirect easily, are "respectful" (i.e., don't "mock" them), and "take them seriously" as "an authority figure." While student behavior is a typical source of stress for preservice teachers (Chaplain, 2008; Horgan et al., 2018), these preservice teachers interpreted these behaviors to mean that these students did not see them as "real" teachers.

Taking Behavior Challenges Less Personally as Time Went On

As time went on in the teacher education program, the preservice teachers started to take challenging student behavior less personally. They would write about noticing their cooperating teachers having similar challenges when addressing student behavior and began to express curiosity about or see the reasons behind student behavior, rather than just describe the behaviors that they found to be stressful. For example, Selena wrote:

> I felt like the same student that had a meltdown is trying to test me. I know not to take it personal, but it is just very frustrating because it is happening with my CT too. Every time I ask what is going on, the student replies with a snarky comment. What could it be?

Here, Selena began to realize that perhaps this student's behavior had nothing to do with her because her cooperating teacher was having similar experiences. Furthermore, Selena demonstrated here that she was beginning to wonder "What could it be?" that caused this student to behave in this way. Alice described a similar moment:

> Some of the kiddos in my class just had a really rough week when it came to managing their own behavior and controlling their bodies/emotions. I think a lot of my students are worried about the [state test] so I am ready for it to mostly be over after next week.

Like Selena, Alice did not take the behavior personally and was curious about why it might be happening, linking these behaviors to the upcoming state test that may have caused her students' "rough week."

Elaine wrote in her journal about student behaviors that she was becoming curious about and believed that her cooperating teacher needed to address:

> I felt unsuccessful when I saw a lot of mean behavior going on between students. They've recently been focusing on self-control and impulse control. One student has been having a hard time controlling his impulses and keeping his hands to himself. He has been sent to the office multiple times for hitting someone else. At this point, I think my CT needs to go back to the basics because they're just being so mean and disrespectful to each other, and no one seems to know why.

As with Alice and Selena, Elaine still felt challenged by student behavior—which, again, is a common challenge and source of stress for preservice teachers (Chaplain, 2008; Horgan et al., 2018), and all three began to take that behavior less personally (e.g., seeing their cooperating teachers also struggle with students' emotional and behavior needs, believing it may be related to state testing, etc.). Elaine took it a step further by expressing that her cooperating teacher may have needed to do some "back to the basics" teaching around respect and kindness.

"Sticking With it" and Offering Themselves Ideas for Next Time

In some instances, these preservice teachers wrote in their journals about opportunities they had to try out some of these ideas and described "sticking with" their ideas without giving up. For example, Sally wrote about a challenging moment with student behavior:

> I had to walk the kids out at the end of the day. They weren't staying in a single file line so it was hard to manage that. I want to learn more of the ways they manage the students at this school.

Rather than end her journal entry after describing her stressful experience walking the kids out at the end of the day, Sally expressed the desire to learn more about how teachers at her field placement school specifically managed routines like walking in the hallway. In this way, she offered herself an idea for something she could do to feel more prepared the next time she walked her class through the hallway (i.e., learn the school's routine). Alycia described a similar experience in her fieldwork journal: "A girl had a meltdown and I felt lost at what to do. I have learned the protocols now." Like Sally, Alycia realized it could be helpful to learn the specific protocols at her school to address such challenges and took the initiative to learn them so she could feel successful the next time she encountered a similar challenge.

Still other preservice teachers described moments in which they "stuck with" whatever attempt they were making at addressing student behavior rather than waiting until after learning the school's protocols (as Sally and Alycia described). Although they described these moments as stressful and challenging, they also felt firsthand how "sticking with it" might be helpful for them when it came to addressing stressful and challenging experiences with student behavior. Bob wrote about one such moment:

> I was taking the kids to lunch but they were talking, turned around, and touching the walls. It took us a total of 10 mins being in line. I tried to wait, I tried to ask for leaders to help, I tried to talk to individual students. However, I ended up having to make at least 3 u-turns for them to finally understand that they weren't meeting my expectations. After this, I re-explained my line expectations. They were upset because they were going to miss their lunch/recess time. I told them that I was hungry too and that I was missing my lunch because the line wasn't the best it could be. They were SHOCKED that I, a human person, ate lunch as well. I think this made them realize that I was missing my lunch time as well so I wasn't doing this to torture them but that I was trying to get them to do their personal best. They lined up really well for the rest of the day and the next day but WHOO. It was a struggle.

Here, Bob expressed in her fieldwork journal that taking the 10 minutes to get her students to the cafeteria was "a struggle," but after connecting with her students and feeling that she "wasn't doing this to torture them," she was able to get them to line up "really well for the rest of the day and the next day."

Quinn wrote about a similar experience with a student who was not listening to her:

> A student did not listen to me several times when I asked him to retry something correctly. He was running and I had to repeat myself several times before he actually did it. Although this made me feel less respected/like a real teacher, I'm happy I continued to follow through without getting upset.

Here, Quinn expressed in her fieldwork journal that even though she had to repeat herself "several times" before her student would "retry" a task "correctly," sticking to her approach by repeating herself ultimately worked. Most importantly, sticking to her plan made her feel "happy" that she "continued to follow through without getting upset."

Supporting Their Students' Social and Emotional Needs Is More Than Behavior Management

There were other incidents that the preservice teachers wrote about in their fieldwork journals about addressing student behaviors in ways that indicated they were concerned about finding ways to support the social and emotional well-being of their students. In these instances, it appeared to feel more important for them to focus on the underlying issues behind their students' behaviors rather than on the presenting behaviors themselves. For example, Maria wrote:

> This week I felt unsuccessful when having to confront a student about talking back. This is a student that needs attention, however, I need to find a new way to support their need while not encouraging negative behaviors. I want this student to develop empathy for their peers and value compassion within themselves.

Here, Maria acknowledged that despite her student's behavior being a challenge for her, she remained committed to supporting him socially and emotionally. Furthermore, she moved beyond feeling overwhelmed by the challenge of his behavior and realized the nuance to the challenges associated with "taking care of children's emotional needs" (Chaplain, 2008; Onchwari, 2010, p. 392). Finally, she extended this even further by sharing her desire to "find a new way to support" her student in this endeavor.

Elaine, who felt her cooperating teacher needed to get "back to basics" to address behavior challenges in her classroom, also began to demonstrate concern for her students' social and emotional well-being in relation to their behaviors. She wrote:

> This week I felt unsuccessful when hearing the words my CT uses to talk to the students. In some instances, she says things that I wouldn't, and it upsets the kids because they feel she's being rude to them. I feel that I need to undo the hurt her words cause and I hope that my kind words will influence her to use kind words.

Elaine experienced some of the stress that role conflict has caused preservice teachers (Zimmerman et al., 2008) when it came to her wanting to "undo the hurt her [cooperating teacher's] words cause[d]" her students. Like Maria, Elaine demonstrated an elevated sense of attention and commitment to the emotional well-being of her students.

Ideas for Addressing Challenging Behavior Became More Prevalent Over Time

As time went on in the teacher education program, others wrote about similar challenges with student behaviors and meeting their field students' social and emotional needs. In some instances, the preservice teachers began to pose questions or ideas to themselves in their fieldwork journals about why this might be happening. For example, Amy wrote:

> A student tried walking away from me because he thought he could get away with it since I am only an intern [i.e., student teacher]. Though some are seeing me as an authority figure, others that I have less contact with, due to intervention and Special Ed pull outs, are testing my fortitude as a teacher. I would have

hoped that they would recognize me as an authority on their own now. This means I need more time with them to show them that, but I am unsure how to do this considering the time constraints.

Amy believed that these particular students may not be responding to her well (i.e., seeing her as a teacher) because she did not have the same amount of contact with them as she did with her other students. Although she expressed frustration and uncertainty, she also expressed that she believed she had identified the problem (i.e., the lack of time together because of "intervention and Special Ed pull outs") and was "hopeful that more time with them" might influence her students to see her "as an authority figure."

Elaine provided a similar rationale when it came to her students not yet seeing her as a teacher early in her field placement:

This week I felt unsuccessful simply because I was the new person in the class and it took a little time for me to be comfortable with being in this new class with older kids, who aren't as excited as pre-K kids. It also took them some time to warm up to me.

Elaine, like Amy, felt that more time would be necessary to establish herself as a teacher in the classroom and that with time, her students might "warm up" to her.

Still other preservice teachers viewed these challenges as learning opportunities, believing the next time they had a similar experience, they might be more prepared. For example, Quinn wrote:

I didn't know a student had an assigned place in line to avoid talking to a friend. Whenever my CT wasn't around, he was sneaking to a new spot and I didn't notice, and it caused lots of disruptions. Finally, my CT noticed him sneaking back to his spot as they approached the classroom. I felt like "G" [pseudonym for field student] felt he could get away with things around me. I made sure to let him know I knew where his spot was now.

Here, Quinn expressed that her student, "G," might not see her as a teacher, and he demonstrated that by "sneaking to a new spot" when her cooperating teacher "wasn't around." However, Quinn took this as an opportunity to establish herself as a teacher by making sure G knew that she knew where he belonged in line, which might help prevent similar "disruptions" in the future.

Maria had a challenging experience with student behavior and was able to get advice from her cooperating teacher about how she might approach such challenges in the future:

This week I felt unsuccessful when monitoring the students outside during recess. Two students got in a verbal fight and I was unsure of which student was telling the truth. I wasn't exactly sure how to handle the situation and I think the students could tell that I was not confident in my decision making. I ended up getting advice from my CT on how to approach this kind of issue in the future.

Here, Maria described not feeling seen as a teacher when she believed her students did not see her as "confident" when addressing their challenging behavior (Chaplain, 2008; Horgan et al., 2018). However, she expressed that her cooperating teacher could be a supportive resource in developing strategies for becoming more confident in her development as a teacher, part of which meant feeling seen as a teacher by students (Murray-Harvey et al., 2000).

ADDRESSING THE STRESS OF MEETING STUDENTS' SOCIAL, EMOTIONAL, AND BEHAVIORAL NEEDS WITH SELF-COMPASSION

Just as they did with their self-compassionate letters about the stressors of delivering academic content to their students, these preservice teachers wrote frequently in their self-compassionate letters about challenges they experienced with student behavior. One key finding in these letters is that many were able to find positives within these challenges that I term "self-compassionate silver linings" (Barry, 2021). May their words encourage you to find self-compassionate silver linings in the challenges you will likely experience when addressing students' complex social, emotional, and behavioral needs.

Excerpts From Educators' Self-Compassionate Letters

Leslie found self-compassionate silver linings in a student's challenging behavior and unique social and emotional needs:

> I know you feel hopeless when you struggle with your student. It's definitely a challenge but just remember that you're doing a great job. Most people would raise their voice, but you are doing a wonderful job at keeping calm. I encourage you to continue to try other ways of communicating with him. This past week you talked on a deeper level and saw another side of him. I think you're definitely on the right track. Keep in mind that not every day will be easy, but that's okay. I don't think he has that many people in his life that treat him with respect, so I'm proud of you for doing so. You are giving him a safe space and allowing him to feel his emotions.

Here, Leslie demonstrated self-compassion in her letter by finding silver linings in the challenges she had while supporting a student emotionally, a common stressor for both preservice teachers (Onchwari, 2010) and experienced teachers (Kelly & Berthelsen, 1995). Rather than be discouraged by the challenge, Leslie focused on how she was successful during this stressful interaction.

Leslie wrote another self-compassionate letter about a moment in which she felt unprepared to support a student's emotional needs:

> One of my students' father passed away 2 weeks before school started + started to cry because she missed him. I didn't know what to do besides hug her + tell her that I love her + am there for her. I was so hard on myself [because] I didn't know what else I could do. Now I realize that I did all I could in the moment and that I can just continue to be a loving + caring person in her life.

What initially felt unsuccessful and caused Leslie to be "hard on" herself because she was not prepared to support that student with the loss of her father shifted to an opportunity to reflect on the experience with mindfulness. Her letter showed that Leslie was able to "realize that [she] did all [she] could in the moment" to support her student and that she did not need to be "hard on" or judge herself for how she responded (Bishop et al., 2004; Kabat-Zinn, 1994; Neff & Germer, 2018; Siegel, 2010).

Elaine also addressed challenging student behavior and her students' complicated social and emotional needs in one of her self-compassionate letters:

> A mon amour,
>
> You are doing a fabulous job! You are focusing on your students + that's what you need to do. Make sure you continue to advocate for your kids. A lot of them have things going on and as a result they'll lash out on you, as the teacher. They don't yet realize that you are there to help + that you are trying to create an environment that allows them to feel a part of a community that cares for them. Kids will lash out but you just have to continue to stay positive and care.
>
> Love, Elaine <3

Elaine was responding mindfully to challenges with her students by encouraging herself to think about the "things going on" in their lives and to remember that "they don't yet realize that [she is] there to help." While this self-compassionate letter is in response to a moment in which she felt unsuccessful in her field placement, Elaine demonstrated mindfulness by taking the judgment off of herself and her students and seeing the situation for what it was (Bishop et al., 2004; Kabat-Zinn, 1994; Neff & Germer, 2018; Siegel, 2010).

Selena showed common humanity in a self-compassionate letter in which she wrote about feeling connected to her students as a learner:

> Hey Selena! First of all, chill out. No one is perfect. It is normal to feel frustrated and angry with a student who is treating others with disrespect. I feel that adults feel like that towards each other too, mostly because we know how feelings are hurt and how they can be impactful. Now that you know how this makes you feel and you have been able to reflect on it, what will you do next time? It may not be a perfect reaction again, but these things take time. No kid does anything on purpose, just like you, they are learning.

Selena's letter is unique here in that she extended the notion of common humanity not to other preservice teachers but to her students when she wrote "just like [her, her students] . . . are learning." As such, just like her, her students are "works-in-progress" (Neff & Germer, 2018, p. 10) with more to learn. Rather than feel isolated for not being "perfect," Selena was "transform[ing her imperfection] into a moment of connection with others" (p. 11) (i.e., her students).

Developing Strong Relationships With Students. Several of the preservice teacher in my dissertation study leaned into the relationships they felt they were building with students when they wrote self-compassionate letters about challenging behavior or students' social and emotional needs. For example, in one of her letters, Bob wrote:

> Dear Bob,
>
> I know the 3rd graders are slightly meaner but be understanding! They can be cute and nice most of the time! Don't let a few bad moments make you feel like it's all bad because YOU KNOW it's not! They're sweet and they love you and you love them! There's only a couple months left with them so be positive and enjoy seeing them while you can! You're going to miss them! Stay strong, be wise, be kind! You've got this!
>
> Love, Bob

Here, Bob did not dismiss the "few bad moments" she had with her students; rather, she reminded herself that despite those moments "they love [her] and [she] love[s] them." In this way, she demonstrated mindfulness by acknowledging her suffering (Bishop et al., 2004; Kabat-Zinn, 1994; Neff & Germer, 2018; Siegel, 2010) and found a self-compassionate silver lining by reminding herself of the strong relationships she felt she was developing with her students despite her stress.

Bob wrote another, similar self-compassionate letter in the middle of the teacher education program:

The Stress of Meeting Students' Social, Emotional, and Behavioral Needs

> Dear Bob,
>
> OH BOY. It's rough and you feel like the kids are really trying to be mean to you but you know they're learning and that they actually love you so don't take the icky stuff to heart! Be good to them and DO NOT give up on them. Believe in them and love them, love them, love them. You've got a great group of kids who are so incredibly sweet and smart. It can feel rough sometimes but it's [be]cause everyone is either tired, grumpy, or hungry. You're all in it together! STAY STRONG. Your break is coming. Be the best Ms. Bob that you can for them. They deserve it!

Here, Bob acknowledged the challenges she had with her students in a similar way to the letter she wrote earlier on in the teacher education program: that she was challenged by their behaviors but that despite these behaviors she still cared for her students and believed they cared for her too. Another self-compassionate silver lining Bob acknowledged in this letter is that her "break [was] coming." While a "break" may be considered more a form of self-care than self-compassion (Corey et al., 2018; Neff & Germer 2018), being a good friend to herself in this moment of suffering (i.e., to be self-compassionate) helped Bob to remind herself that she would soon have time for a break.

More Self-Compassionate Silver Linings to Student Behavior and Seeking Out Help. This trend of finding and writing about self-compassionate silver linings and encouraging themselves to get help continued in several of these preservice teachers' self-compassionate letters as they continued to progress through the teacher education program. For example, Amy wrote:

> So a kid decided to rage quit when you asked them to fix something. . . . Big deal! Lol . . . just kidding. But seriously, the situation escalated so quickly, it is no wonder why you didn't know how to handle it. You never faced anything like that before. Letting your CT handle the fallout ensured that the situation would not be made worse by being involved. You were able to give your input, and leave the rest to the person most familiar with these things. And even she wasn't able to fix it! The woman who knows so much about classroom management wasn't able to. You did your best!

Here, Amy acknowledged that she had never faced a challenge with student behavior like the one she wrote about. Additionally, she described it as an opportunity to learn from her cooperating teacher how to handle that situation by having her "handle the fallout." Furthermore, to see her cooperating teacher not be "able to fix it" despite how much she "knows . . . about classroom management" seemed to be a great learning opportunity for Amy: that everyone—including the most experienced teachers—experience challenges (Neff, 2011; Neff & Germer, 2018).

Bob encouraged herself to seek out help in one of her self-compassionate letters when she wrote:

Bob,

LOOK. These kids are testing you. Don't take it personally! They are learning that you're not messing around! Plus, you love them. It'll be great! I know it feels scary not knowing what to do but STAY STRONG! You can only grow from here! You are loved and you can do this! STAY STRONG! Finish strong! Do some fun stuff and ask for help! DUDE. ASK. FOR. HELP!!! It's Okay! Pride is so dumb! You're a forever learner. Stay loving, stay strong!
LOVE YOU!

Bob <3

Here, Bob realized that to ask for help might be a way to address those challenging feelings rather than to suffer alone. In her words, "[p]ride is so dumb!"

Write Your Own Self-Compassionate Letter That Addresses the Stress of Meeting Students' Social, Emotional, and Behavioral Needs

Student behavior, classroom management, and social and emotional needs are such common sources of stress for teachers at any career stage. For me, meeting those needs was something that I got better at, but throughout my teaching career, these were the challenges that continued to come up. I found that when I was presented with a behavior challenge or faced with a student's unique social and emotional needs, I'd need to get creative and go back to the drawing board more often than I would with any of the other stressors I experienced as a teacher. There is an incredible amount of nuance to every child's situation that makes it hard to know how to help right away. You need time to get to know the student and their unique needs in ways that, to me, were more time-consuming and draining than learning to teach content to students who were struggling academically.

With this in mind, complete the following exercise, which will lead into writing a self-compassionate letter about dealing with challenging student behaviors and meeting their social and emotional needs. As with all the exercises in this book, they have been adapted from Neff's (2011) "Exploring Self-Compassion Through Letter Writing" to reflect the unique challenges and stressors that new and developing teachers experience.

1. Consider this question: Do you have a classmate or colleague that you feel close to, either in your teacher education program or at your school? If yes, I want you to picture that person right now. If you don't have someone like that, it's ok; instead, imagine

someone else in your life that you feel close to or imagine someone that you could feel close to.
2. Now, imagine that your dear friend from your teacher education program or your colleague at your school—real or imaginary—confided in you that they didn't know how to handle a student's challenging behavior. They express to you that they're feeling overwhelmed and exhausted by trying to balance this student's social and emotional needs and the needs of other students in their class.
    » What would you tell them about challenging behaviors with students?
    » How would you convey to them that even the best routines and behavior management systems don't always work?
    » How would you remind them that their abilities as a teacher are not solely defined by their students' challenging behaviors?
    » How would you demonstrate compassion for this friend if there is an aspect of their identity that makes meeting students' social and emotional needs more challenging?
    » Would you remind them that most developing teachers struggle with behavior management and that most teachers cite meeting their students' social and emotional needs as one of the biggest challenges they face even after years of teaching experience?
3. Now, take some time to write your letter. Think about a time when you didn't know how to handle a student's challenging behavior. Reflect on what you thought about *what you would say to your friend or colleague* in steps 1 and 2 and how you would encourage them while dealing with challenging student behaviors and social-emotional needs. Begin writing a letter to convey what you would tell them. However, instead of addressing the letter to the real or imagined friend, address it to yourself.

Example: My Self-Compassionate Letter About Losing Scott on the First Day of School

Dear Dave,

Even all these years later, I still remember how scared you were when you thought Scott was lost on your first day as a classroom teacher. I remember how inadequate you felt and how certain you were that you would lose your job. The stress, fear, and concern you felt on that first day would be how anyone would feel if they were in your shoes at any point in their teaching career. It was a terrible situation that fortunately had a happy ending.

I know to this day you still feel some responsibility for what happened, which is an understandable feeling. I want to remind you, though, that you were where you were supposed to be—waiting with the students who were being picked up by their families at the end of the day—and you could not have been there to make sure that Scott stayed where he was supposed to. The first day of school's dismissal is always chaotic, and I'm sure that whoever was monitoring the students in their bus line was frantically herding the 20+ students that they had just met for the first time minutes before. The bus driver probably assumed that the person who brought Scott and that pre-K student onto the bus checked each of their bus tags ahead of time, which they did, but did so as they were entering the auditorium for dismissal and unfortunately not as they were getting on to the bus. Although it is the adults' job to keep children safe at school, teachers and bus drivers are just people, and people make mistakes. This was a really unfortunate and frightening mistake, but it's important to remember that at no point were Scott and his pre-K partner in any danger.

Despite how scary this was, there were things that you and the greater community did to address it that ensured that Scott and the pre-K student were safe. You had a lot of anxiety about being new and believed that families didn't think a new, young, male kindergarten teacher was capable of doing all the things a kindergarten teacher needs to do like teach effectively and keep children safe. This felt like you were proving your worries right when you couldn't keep Scott safe, and that must have been really hard. All that said, thank goodness you and your assistant put so much time and effort into creating those bus tags! Those included the bus and bus stop they were supposed to get on and off at, as well as the school's address and phone number. Second, thank goodness for those families who realized Scott and the pre-K student were in the wrong place and took the initiative as school community members to flag down the police officer who would return them to school safely.

I'm not sure that there is much you could've done differently, Dave, and I know that might not be easy to digest. It did make you appreciate the greater school community and realize that there are some students that need to be monitored more closely in these large, chaotic situations. You didn't know Scott well enough yet to know that he needed a closer eye on him than other students, and you learned from that experience how to recognize behaviors that other students might demonstrate in the future when they need to be more closely monitored (e.g., have someone hold their hand at all times).

You didn't write about this, but I want to remind you that later in the school year, Scott began to thrive and truly saw you as a caregiver. I remember that time he dropped from the monkey bars and scared himself (and you). He walked right to you, crying, and you asked if he wanted you to carry him or hold his hand on the way to the nurse's office, and he said "carry me." Scott knew that you cared about him.

Love,
Dave

CHAPTER 5

The Stress of Relationship Dynamics With Cooperating Teachers, School Staff, Families, and Teacher Educators

> Challenges With My Cooperating Teacher
> (Author's Student Teaching Journal, 2/5/2007)
>
> I'm starting to get concerned about a few things. I love my cooperating teacher, but now that I've taken over a lot of her class, she feels somewhat out of place. During meeting time, I'll ask questions, and instead of letting the kids answer my questions, she'll ask it again, sometimes different and sometimes not, and starts giving them hints. The kids then turn around to her because they're used to her, and then kind of makes it seem like I can't handle the class when they start talking to her, telling them "you need to listen to Mr. Barry," confusing them even more.
>
> I think a lot of it is because I'm the first student teacher she's had and has never had to really share a class with anyone before. Hopefully, when [my field supervisor] comes tomorrow she'll be able to see that and facilitate a conversation about it.

MY OWN CHALLENGES MANAGING RELATIONSHIP DYNAMICS WITH COOPERATING TEACHERS, SCHOOL STAFF, FAMILIES, AND TEACHER EDUCATORS

The vignette above from my student teaching journal demonstrates another common challenge experienced by preservice teachers: relationship dynamics with cooperating teachers, school staff, families, and teacher educators (Murray-Harvey et al., 2000; Zimmerman, 2008). The challenge for me came during my takeover week in pre-K when my cooperating teacher and I struggled to find our place as our roles changed.

WHY ARE RELATIONSHIP DYNAMICS WITH COOPERATING TEACHERS, SCHOOL STAFF, FAMILIES, AND TEACHER EDUCATORS STRESSFUL FOR PRESERVICE TEACHERS?

Many of the preservice teachers wrote in their fieldwork journals about moments in which they felt unsure about their cooperating teacher's expectations, ranging from uncertainty about their role as a preservice teacher in their cooperating teacher's classroom (Zimmerman et al., 2008), to uncertainty about classroom rules and routines in which they had not yet developed fluency. Previous scholarship indicates that the relationship between preservice teachers and their cooperating teachers is an important factor in determining a preservice teacher's experience with stress (Murray-Harvey et al., 2000). When preservice teachers determine that the relationship is a positive one, they tend to feel less stressed in their field placements. However, when they perceive the relationship to be negative or strained, preservice teachers tend to report higher levels of stress (p. 32). What follows are examples of the ways in which some of these preservice teachers felt unsure of their cooperating teachers' expectations, which led to several instances where they reported feeling stressed.

Dynamics With Cooperating Teachers

Nicole reflected in her fieldwork journal about her uncertainty regarding her cooperating teacher's expectations of her:

> I felt unsuccessful when I was trying to figure out my role in the classroom with [my cooperating teacher]. I think my fellow [student] teachers can say the same. It is hard to know what to do exactly in a given situation when one of your students is acting up and whether or not I should talk to them or allow [my cooperating teacher] to. No one wants to step on their CT's [cooperating teacher's] shoes at all because this is their classroom and students. I would like clarification in what seems like the appropriate things to do are.

Here, Nicole expressed what previous researchers have termed "role conflict": a preservice teacher's feeling of uncertainty about what their role in the classroom is and what their cooperating teacher expects the preservice teacher's role in their classroom should be (Horgan et al., 2018; Zimmerman et al., 2008).

Several of the preservice teachers expressed similar feelings of uncertainty about their role in their field classrooms. For example, Quinn wrote:

> I still feel like I am sometimes unfamiliar with the procedures or rules, or lack the ability to follow through when a student is having a behavioral issue, so I

feel that I still need my CT to step in often and that makes me feel less like a real teacher. It makes me feel less capable and like I'm not good at what I'm doing.

For Quinn, not knowing what to do when addressing student behavior was a challenge (Chaplain, 2008; Horgan et al., 2018), and she connected that experience of not knowing what to do in this situation to not feeling like "a real teacher" because she needed her cooperating teacher to "step in" and take over.

In some instances, the preservice teachers made attempts to take the lead in their cooperating teachers' classrooms when it came to giving students directions. Unfortunately, their directions did not always align with their cooperating teachers' expectations, routines, and classroom rules. In fact, in their fieldwork journals, they described scenarios where they took the lead and students ended up being reprimanded by the cooperating teacher for following the preservice teacher's "wrong" directions. In these moments of reported stress, the preservice teachers felt simultaneously unsupported by their cooperating teachers (Murray-Harvey et al., 2000) and uncertain about their cooperating teachers' expectations (Horgan et al. 2018; Zimmerman et al., 2008). For example, Sally wrote:

> This week in my field placement, I felt unsuccessful when . . . I gave them wrong directions. I feel as if I am still learning my boundaries in the classroom of what I can and can't do. I ended up giving a whole table the wrong directions regarding an assignment and they got reprimanded by the teacher.

Sally's attempt at taking the lead in her field classroom (i.e., giving directions) resulted in her students being "reprimanded" by her cooperating teacher for Sally's mistake. In this moment, she expressed her uncertainty about what she "can and can't do" in the classroom, mirroring previous research on preservice teachers' experiences of stress related to role conflict (Horgan et al., 2018; Zimmerman et al., 2008).

Nora wrote about a similar experience giving her students the wrong directions and witnessing them being reprimanded by her cooperating teacher:

> This week in my field placement, I felt unsuccessful when . . . I wasn't sure when the teacher liked the students to go to the bathroom and drink water, and I didn't know which students made it a habit to drink water multiple times so I let them go and [my cooperating teacher] would yell at them to sit down and they would say "but Ms. Nora said I could." This made me feel like I was ruining the rules of the classroom, but [my cooperating teacher] later told me that I should do what I feel is right and take assertiveness. That made me feel comfortable that [my cooperating teacher] was allowing me to . . . give out permission to students to do things.

Although Nora's mistake resulted in her students being reprimanded by her cooperating teacher in ways similar to Sally, Nora expressed that her bond with her cooperating teacher eased her stress when she was given permission to do what she felt was "right" in the classroom (Murray-Harvey et al., 2000). Without a follow-up conversation with her cooperating teacher to encourage her to take an active role in the classroom, Sally's relationship with her cooperating teacher (Murray-Harvey et al., 2000) and unresolved role conflict (Zimmerman et al., 2008) may have persisted as sources of stress for her.

Clare, a field supervisor who supported many of these preservice teachers in their field placements, described the pressure they felt to not "mess up for their CT" when we spoke in an interview:

> I think there's a lot of uncertainty that goes with being a beginner at something and knowing that you are a beginner. That uncertainty is really connected to knowing that what you're doing is really important. So I mean, they, they don't want to mess up for their cooperating teachers, you know, how their, their kids are going to do on standardized testing and things like that. So that, you know, wanting to be really careful to not make mistakes and do the best they can in those kinds of circumstances, I think, is something that they're concerned about as well.

Clare was describing the pressure these preservice teachers felt to not make mistakes because of the negative impact such mistakes would have on their relationship with their cooperating teacher and their students' performance on state-mandated standardized tests. She expressed how those feelings about making mistakes or being ineffective with students not only made them feel ineffective as teachers but could make them worry that they may be letting down their cooperating teachers when they made mistakes.

Alice described a moment that echoed Clare's comments when she wrote in her fieldwork journal:

> My CT spoke harshly to me while I was trying to help a student. The child was not following instructions and was disrupting the class. They knocked over a box of markers. I walked over to clean up the markers. My CT sternly told me to not touch the markers. She wanted the student who made the mess to clean it up. I understood this, but her tone caught me off guard. In that instance, I felt as though I too was a student in the class. I was back in kindergarten being told what to do. I did not feel a lot of agency in this classroom. Instead, I feel like sometimes I am merely following instructions.

Alice felt that being spoken to so "harshly" and "sternly" by her cooperating teacher made her feel they saw her not as a teacher, but as one of the kindergarten students in her class. Similar to how these preservice teachers and the students they worked with experienced role conflict (Zimmerman et al., 2008) regarding who they were in their classrooms, Alice's cooperating teacher expressed a similar conflict regarding Alice's role in her classroom. Additionally, being spoken to by her cooperating teacher in this way could have been damaging to their relationship, illuminating another potential—and common—source of stress that preservice teachers report experiencing while enrolled in teacher education programs (Murray-Harvey et al., 2000).

Maria described a moment in her journal about the challenging relationship dynamics with her cooperating teacher. Specifically, she reflected on her belief that she needed more opportunities to teach in order to increase her cooperating teacher's confidence in her as a teacher:

> This week I felt unsuccessful when my CT did not seem confident in allowing me to teach more large group lessons in the classroom. I would really want more opportunities to get experience teaching, however there does not seem to be a lot of time in this second-grade teaching schedule. All of the second-grade teachers create the exact same lesson plans that they share together. This is efficient but does not allow for a lot of flexibility for individual teachers. I hope that I get more opportunities to teach lessons throughout the semester.

Alycia described a similar experience: "My CT allowed me to lead the class activity and I messed up and forgot to say everything he told me to and he had to step in." Alycia also brought up her challenging relationship with her cooperating teacher during an interview:

> I think in the field it's more like me not wanting to step on my CT's toes or interfere with the lessons because he has two classes of each thing and I'm trying to do my work in that and not disturbing [him]. If I mess one class up or what the next class is going to do, it can throw one class off their schedule and stuff. This last past week, I had to do an observation and it was Bingo, and it was only with the advanced group. So that helped because they'll catch up. But I don't know what I would've done if it was the on-level group, because if I would've thrown them off with testing right now, [my cooperating teacher is] already on a time crunch and I don't want to be stepping on his toes or whatever. That makes me nervous.

Here, Alycia expressed that she needed to get practice teaching and that this practice needed to be observed and evaluated by her field supervisor in order to meet the requirements of the teacher education program. However, she felt "nervous" about "stepping on" her cooperating teacher's "toes" by needing these experiences teaching and being observed because of a rigid schedule and state-mandated testing (Facchinetti, 2010; Horgan et al., 2018). Like Maria, if Alycia continued to feel that her relationship with her cooperating teacher was strained, it is likely that both preservice teachers would continue to feel "nervous" or stressed in ways similar to other preservice teachers experiencing this stressor (Murray-Harvey et al., 2000).

There were also instances where the preservice teachers felt caught off guard by their cooperating teachers' critiques. For example, Elaine wrote:

> It was difficult for me to find my confidence to be in the front of the class and speak. I had to force myself to do it, which actually helped me a lot. Towards the end of the week I felt more confident in front of the class. I also felt unsuccessful when my CT told me that I seemed disconnected from what I was talking about. The advice was really helpful and I've been trying to seem more involved and more connected, but it's really hard when you think you are.

While Elaine found her cooperating teacher's advice "really helpful," the help she received did not seem constructive (Costa et al., 2016; Murray-Harvey et al., 2000; Wetzel et al., 2017), as it seemed to blindside her.

Elaine wrote about another moment in which she felt she had been successful teaching her students but her cooperating teacher did not agree:

> I reviewed integer operations with [my field students] and it took a little extra time and we weren't able to start their game until the next day, but I thought the lesson went well because a lot of students who didn't understand before understood now. Then I was told that it didn't go well at all and that the students were being disrespectful and that the lesson took too long and just all of these things that I didn't notice, which also worried my CT. I think the thing that bothered me the most was that she said she thinks I'm just unaware, which made me feel like I had no place in a classroom.

Although Elaine was able to pinpoint what was successful about her teaching (e.g., "a lot of students who didn't understand before understood now"), her cooperating teacher saw it differently. In fact, Elaine believed her cooperating teacher thought Elaine was "just unaware." It's hard to know exactly what happened in this interaction, but how it made Elaine feel is important to honor. If made to feel she "had no place in a classroom" after this interaction with her cooperating teacher, Elaine may not have perceived her relationship with her cooperating teacher as positive, which could have led to higher levels of the stress she experienced as a preservice teacher (Murray-Harvey et al., 2000).

Quinn described a moment in her fieldwork journal in which she felt her cooperating teacher was not supportive, even though Quinn had previously felt supported by this cooperating teacher:

> I asked my CT how to specifically differentiate for a student with a learning disability. She seemed exasperated with me and was like "I don't know, you're the

teacher!" It made me feel foolish for asking, like I am not independent enough. I just really didn't want to make a poor decision for the child.

Although Quinn previously had experiences with this cooperating teacher in which she felt supported through team teaching by "modeling expert thinking and problem-solving processes" (Costa et al., 2016, Kindle Locations 537–539), her reaction to Quinn's plea for help made her "feel foolish for asking," which, as Quinn experienced, showed a lack of emotional support. As Wetzel et al. (2017) wrote, "[e]xpertise is certainly an important resource for a mentor, but the social and emotional work of mentoring is just as important" (p. 10). For Quinn, having the technical support but not the emotional support from her cooperating teacher made her feel unsuccessful.

Quinn described in a later fieldwork journal that she wanted to have a stronger relationship with her cooperating teacher so she could be more honest about the struggles she was experiencing as a preservice teacher:

I called in [sick] because I was way too overwhelmed by the end of the week. I felt disappointed in myself, but also my brain was not in the right space to be handling that classroom all by myself. I wish my relationship with my CT was at a place where I felt comfortable just being honest with her and asking for help, but I have heard her make disparaging comments about teachers with mental health struggles before and I am afraid of seeming weak around her, to the point where I would rather be dishonest and say that I am sick.

Quinn's previous negative experience when she asked this cooperating teacher for help may have contributed to her concerns about asking for more help and "just being honest" about her "mental health struggles." While Quinn's cooperating teacher had previously expressed her willingness to support Quinn's teaching (e.g., team teaching), Quinn did not believe that her cooperating teacher would support her emotionally if she appeared "weak" given the "disparaging comments" her cooperating teacher made to her about "teachers with mental health struggles." As researchers have found, emotional support is an important aspect of this relationship (Wetzel et al., 2017) that has been shown to reduce stress among preservice teachers (Murray-Harvey et al., 2000). For Quinn, it seemed that this kind of support was not available to her, perhaps making her experience in her cooperating teacher's classroom more stressful.

The cooperating teachers, however, were not the only adults in the school community with whom there were documented stressful relationship dynamics. Particularly in challenging and stressful moments that took place outside of the classroom (e.g., cafeteria, hallway, etc.), they described several experiences in which they felt other teachers and administrators did not see them as teachers.

Dynamics With Other Teachers and Administrators

Tamara described an experience in which she was "criticized" by another teacher:

> The other Pre-K teacher criticized me for helping one of the students in my placement classroom. My CT was running late, so the other teacher and I were walking the classes down the hall together to the cafeteria for breakfast. One of the students was struggling to put her jacket in her backpack as we walked, so I helped her unzip the backpack and put her jacket in so that she could continue. The teacher came around the corner and scolded me for helping her, emphasizing that "we're supposed to be letting them do stuff themselves." I was allowing her to try and complete the task on her own, but, when it was clear that she couldn't walk and open her backpack at the same time, as the teacher was insisting, I stepped in and offered her my assistance.

Leslie had a similar stressful moment in which she felt other teachers did not see her as a teacher:

> We were walking in the hall and one student lay on the ground and stayed there. He did not get up when I asked. I felt like my CT thought I could not handle him. I was also very embarrassed because more teachers saw him laying down and ignoring me.

Feeling that after this incident her cooperating teacher would believe Leslie "could not handle" the student and feeling "embarrassed" that other teachers saw this student "ignoring" her directions connects with previous literature on preservice teachers' experiences with stress, namely, the challenges of student behavior (Chaplain, 2008; Horgan et al., 2018). Leslie's experience extends this literature to include how she believes other school staff—not just Leslie—conceived of her ability to manage student behavior. Perceiving that her cooperating teacher and other teachers did not believe she could handle the situation may also have added to the stress she experienced as a preservice teacher.

Amy described a similar experience in which she attempted to manage student behavior outside of the classroom: "I was unable to bring [a student] back into the classroom. Another teacher walking by was able to do so with what seemed like very little effort." For Amy, the stress of this moment seemed to be tied to two things: her belief that a student did not see her as a real teacher and her feeling that another teacher saw her as incapable of managing student behavior and deciding to intervene. Although this may have been a friendly attempt to support Amy, it made her feel unsuccessful to see another teacher be able to manage a challenging situation with a student with what Amy perceived to be "very little effort."

There were also incidents in which these preservice teachers described stressful moments in which they felt their school administrators did not see them as capable. Nora reflected on one such moment:

> My CT let me take the girls to the bathroom outside in the hallway to change for ballet. The girls were really loud and I could not get them to be quiet. Mr. G the principal, was having a meeting right next door and I knew he was not happy. He came outside [and] got them to be quiet in an instant.

Again, these moments of feeling incapable of managing challenging student behaviors are commonly reported stressors among preservice teachers (Chaplain, 2008; Horgan et al., 2018). However, preservice teachers like Leslie, Tamara, Nora, and Amy experienced additional layers of stress when dealing with student behavior when other teachers or administrators saw them be unsuccessful in these moments and intervened. While some cooperating teachers took these opportunities to reinforce that these preservice teachers should trust their instincts and made them feel like they could continue to try (e.g., Nora's cooperating teacher after Nora allowed children to go to the bathroom at the "wrong" time), other cooperating teachers, other teachers, and administrators did not seem to take many opportunities to have conversations with these preservice teachers after these stressful incidents with students occurred, leaving them to feel stressed, unsuccessful, and as if they were not seen as teachers by the people who were meant to support them in becoming teachers. This lack of support is evident in the limited extant research on preservice teachers' stress (Chaplain, 2008; Horgan et al., 2018).

Cara wrote in her fieldwork journal about a challenging experience working with a substitute teacher:

> The sub was undermining my authority during the day and would make comments to the kids to make it seem like they didn't have to listen to me. At one point I had told a student they couldn't do something and then the student asked the sub and the sub told the student they could. I hope it was not intentional, but it did not feel good.

Feeling "undermin[ed]" by the substitute teacher made Cara feel that this substitute teacher did not see her as a teacher, which indirectly reinforced to her students that she was not a capable teacher.

Maria described feeling unsuccessful when she attempted to walk her class quietly through the hallway while other students were taking the state test:

> This week I felt unsuccessful when walking the students to lunch because our class was rowdy and loud. The students needed to be particularly quiet due to the

older grades taking the state test. I felt particularly worried when my students were loud because I didn't want to disturb the students that were working hard on their exams.

Managing student behavior (i.e., getting the class to be quiet) is a common source of stress for preservice teachers (Chaplain, 2008; Horgan et al., 2018); however, Maria's "worr[y]" about how "rowdy and loud" her class was in the hallways was amplified by how it could impact other students who were taking a test.

Sally had an experience in which another teacher stepped in to help her with her students:

> My CT was gone the very first rotation, the kids wouldn't pack up quick enough and another teacher came in to help. I feel like I could've gotten them to go if I had more time but the teacher wanted them to go faster.

Here, Sally expressed frustration that the other teacher intervened, believing she was capable of getting her students to "pack up." In this way, she felt unsuccessful because this other teacher took away an opportunity that Sally was developing confidence in by intervening. In Sally's case, the positive was that she *believed* she was capable of successfully managing a transition, which was a source of stress many of these preservice wrote about in their fieldwork journals throughout the teacher education program.

Quinn wrote about a stressful experience with her grade-level teammates in her fieldwork journal:

> Another teacher on my team had me plan an entire unit for social studies even though it is her only team responsibility. I spent about 16 hours on it, and put off doing other necessary things. Then she decided she "didn't like the textbook" and that I needed to come up with a completely different unit. Which I did. Then I see that she ended up just doing the first one. I am very frustrated, feeling used and not respected. I just want to feel like an equal part of the team but instead I get treated like everyone's personal assistant. I know my time is worth more than that, but I can't find the courage to say no or speak up for myself.

Although Quinn described wanting to "feel like an equal part of the team," her attempt at supporting her colleague made her feel "used and not respected" and as if she were "everyone's personal assistant" rather than a teacher. Further, as time is a significant source of stress for preservice teachers (Facchinetti, 2010; Horgan et al., 2018), the 16 hours she spent planning this social studies unit may have added an additional layer of stress to the situation she described in her journal.

Dynamics With Students' Parents

When it came to challenging relationships for these preservice teachers, a new school community member, the parent, emerged in some of their fieldwork journals. I didn't find other examples of stressful interactions with parents and families in the literature as common sources of stress for preservice teachers (Barry, 2021); however, challenges with parents are common stressors for teachers (Yong & Yue, 2007, p. 81). Next, I will share my own experience dealing with a stressful relationship with families during my first year of teaching.

> I was incredibly lucky my first year of teaching to be paired with a teacher mentor; she was in fact the retired teacher I'd been hired to replace. The woman who had been her assistant for over a decade agreed to be my assistant to aid me in learning the kindergarten ropes. I also am very aware how lucky I was to have a full-time assistant, as that is not always the practice in kindergarten classrooms. I was also on a team of truly talented kindergarten teachers who really wanted to help me be successful. When it came to support, I was incredibly fortunate. I still had no idea what I was doing or what to even ask most of the time, but I could go to them with anything, and they would help me.
>
> I remember that my students' parents were for the most part really excited that a young, male, musical person (i.e., me) was going to be their child's teacher. There were a few parents, however, that were very concerned that I was so new and wouldn't be capable of teaching their children effectively. Because I had already decided that I didn't know what I was doing and that I wasn't a real teacher, their opinions of me—even though it was just a few of them—became the voices in my head that I believed proved me right; I wasn't a teacher, I was an imposter.
>
> I remember several occasions that first year where my students weren't following in their lines or were talking in the hallway and another teacher would come over to manage them on my behalf. I would thank them, but inside it only reinforced that I wasn't a good teacher and I had no control. Other times things would get loud in my class because the children were playing in their centers and another teacher would pop their head in to make sure everything was okay. These check-ins would, again, make me feel that I wasn't the only person who didn't think I could be a teacher—maybe my colleagues thought so too.
>
> The concerns about how other adults saw me as a teacher made me feel like I had to be tougher and stricter with my students. The teacher I imagined myself as—a sort of Maria von Trapp with attentive students sitting around my feet while I sang to them with my guitar—was being taken over by more of an Oscar the Grouch. I felt like I had to raise my voice when other teachers were around so that they would take me seriously and believe I had control of the behaviors they thought weren't appropriate for kindergarteners. I didn't like who I was as a teacher a lot that first

> *year as a result of my concerns about how other adults in the building might see me as a teacher.*

Although I was unable to find examples in the literature of challenging relationship dynamics between preservice teachers and families (Barry, 2021), a few preservice teachers in the study guiding this book identified that relationships with parents were stressful.

For example, Cara wrote:

> During Outdoor School, there were a few medical emergencies going on at the same time that caused the 3 fifth grade teachers to be occupied, so it made me the "next" person in charge. The kids were acting a little wild during a game they were playing, and a parent was harsh and told me I did not have control and needed to do something and that this is the worst she had seen. I felt unsuccessful because I didn't know what to do, and I didn't agree with the parent.

Amy also described a challenging experience with one of her student's parents when she wrote, "A parent came to my CT to complain about how I handled a disciplinary situation. I ended up crying in front of my CT and Ms. K the math teacher." Although Amy attempted to manage "a disciplinary situation" on her own by using her own teacher decision-making process to do so (Borko & Cadwell, 1982), it was met with critique from a parent (Yong & Yue, 2007) and led her to cry in front of other teachers. For Amy, it seemed that having her discipline decision critiqued by a parent and crying in front of other teachers was an incredibly challenging and stressful experience.

Dynamics With Teacher Educators

It came up in every interview I conducted with every participant—the preservice teachers, their field supervisors, and their cohort coordinators—that the teacher education program was generally very stressful for preservice teachers and that they needed more support than they were getting to manage that stress (Barry, 2021). Although researchers have found that teacher education programs can be very challenging for preservice teachers, particularly early in the program (Murray-Harvey et al., 2000), it feels important to illuminate a less often discussed relationship in the teacher education program these participants found to be particularly stressful: preservice teachers' relationships with teacher educators.

The preservice teachers in this study described several instances in which they felt their teacher educators (i.e., cohort coordinators, field supervisors, and professors) were not consistent in their support, or that their support was contingent on fulfilling expectations. For example, in Selena's first interview, she said:

> So, a lot of the time it's as if our professors say "we're here for you, we know that everyone goes through things. Oh, but if you miss a day, you have a five-page essay and you're getting five points off of your grade." And yesterday, it was kind of sad to hear my friend, one of the people in the cohort, her boyfriend's dad is like in critical care in the hospital and apparently the hospital called him last night and was like, "hey, you know you should come over here." And of course she really wanted to be there with him, but she was like, "well do I go? Because we have class tomorrow and they're going to get mad at me or they're gonna like make me write an essay." And she said "I wish this happened on Monday because then I would be able to miss my placement with no problem and just make it up." I was like, "wow, you know, you're right." Our CTs get it, like, "hey, things happen. I take days off." The fact that we would rather take time out of our placement rather than our classes I think says a lot about like the message our professors send to us in terms of the limitations on taking care of ourselves and what that looks like to them.

Here, Selena expressed that having an understanding cooperating teacher made it easier to manage the stressors that exist outside the teacher education program (Murray-Harvey et al., 2000). However, from her perspective, this supportive relationship did not appear to exist consistently between these preservice teachers and their course instructors.

Maria, in her second interview, which occurred after she graduated and had her own classroom, also described the inconsistency in the support she felt she and the other preservice teachers received from their course instructors:

> Yeah, there's some weird irony there with like, the professors are trying to support us in the best way possible, but then at the same time, it's like, "we need these grades in and we have this much time." And so, it's weird that we're supposed to be incorporating SEL [social–emotional learning] into all of our lessons, but it's definitely not valued in the [teacher education program], you know? Because it's not really always incorporated.

Like Selena, Maria experienced inconsistent messaging from her professors and instructors about the contingencies of their support. Further, Maria found it ironic that they, as preservice teachers, were expected to incorporate social–emotional learning (SEL) in their lessons while her professors did not afford the preservice teachers the same opportunities for social–emotional support in their own coursework. These findings are similar to those found by Brown et al. (2020) in which preservice teachers described the inconsistencies between how they were taught to teach children and how they were taught by their teacher educators.

Like Maria and Selena, Amy also believed there was inconsistency in the support she and her fellow preservice teachers received from their course instructors. She said in her first interview:

> I think back to last semester [semester 1], and I hate to throw my teachers under the bus, I loved them, and they would tell us how much they supported us and how much they understood what we were going through and then they'd lay on the work. The work did not lessen up even slightly, in fact, it would just get heavier. So it was that kind of, uh, it was not following through with your words.

The stress Maria, Selena, and Amy experienced with their instructors was connected to the ways they perceived their professors would express awareness of their stress and support them verbally, but not follow through with any tangible actions to demonstrate that support (e.g., reducing assignments, being flexible when life circumstances interfere with attendance, etc.).

Others described a lack of flexibility from their course instructors. For example, Anna said in her second interview:

> It was more so challenging I think during semester one. Semester one was much more, it just seemed like the workload was a lot heavier. I remember talking with the professors in semester one, especially the, I guess it was one of the language arts courses. We tried to talk to the professors, but the professors weren't giving much. Like they just kind of held to "these are the expectations. You can meet them. There are enough hours in the day."

Although Anna attempted to talk with her professors about the "heav[y]" workload in one of her courses—a common stressor for preservice teachers (Chaplain, 2008; Horgan et al., 2018)—Alycia described feeling "afraid" to tell her teacher educators about inflexible professors during semester 1 because she worried it would get back to the professor:

> I feel like in semester one it was really like we needed someone to be our voice. Like there was a lot of like things happening that a lot of professors, like we would tell it to one, but we were afraid they were going to tell someone else. So we didn't want them to know how we felt actually about another professor or like we just didn't want to step on anyone's toes I guess.

For Alycia, having "someone to be [their] voice" who could communicate on the preservice teachers' behalf would have helped her feel less stressed about who she could talk to safely regarding her concerns without fear of retaliation.

Amy also described how important it was to have someone supportive in the teacher education program—she believed that was their cohort coordinator, Nana—in light of feeling unsupported by her teacher educators:

> All of our teachers, they tell you, "Oh, we understand it's a lot. And we understand it's really hard to do it all. And some of you might not do it all," but then they wouldn't, they wouldn't adjust when we talked. When we would tell them just how overwhelmed we are and that we can't get it done, that it is humanly impossible unless they want us to not sleep at night, some of them didn't adjust anything. They left it the exact same. So, it was a disconnect between what they would say and what they would do. As far as support that really helped in the TEP [teacher education program], it was the really understanding people like Nana. She's amazing. I'm sure that's what everyone would say 'cause she, if we had problems, we would go to her, and if she couldn't fix it, at least we would talk it out or she'd give us some strategy.

Amy's comments point to the irony or hypocrisy the other preservice teachers described; however, she did feel supported by her cohort coordinator, Nana, when she and her fellow preservice teachers experienced challenges.

ADDRESSING THE STRESS OF MANAGING RELATIONSHIP DYNAMICS WITH COOPERATING TEACHERS, SCHOOL STAFF, FAMILIES, AND TEACHER EDUCATORS WITH SELF-COMPASSION

Several preservice teachers in this study expressed feeling stressed about their relationships with adults in their school communities (cooperating teachers, other teachers, administrators, and parents) and in their courses in the teacher education program (teacher educators) in their interviews and in their journals. However, the only adults connected to the teacher education program they wrote self-compassionate letters about regarding stressful relationship were their cooperating teachers (Barry, 2021). As a researcher, this signals to me that of all the professional adult relationships that can cause stress throughout a teacher education program, the relationship with the cooperating teacher has the potential to be the most stressful (e.g., Murray-Harvey et al., 2000). Therefore, other than the relationship dynamics with their students, it appeared in the data I was able to collect and analyze that a preservice teacher's relationship with the cooperating teacher may be the relationship that requires the most self-compassion in preservice teacher education programs (Barry, 2021). What follows are examples of self-compassionate letters in which these preservice teachers addressed stress in their relationships with their cooperating teachers.

Excerpts From Educators' Self-Compassionate Letters

Sally wrote a self-compassionate letter about a stressful experience with her cooperating teacher:

> Dear Sally,
>
> My friend—never feel as if you are not enough. You have all the knowledge you need to be where you are standing. Your empathy and love will shine through all that you do. You made one small mistake but do not let that overshadow all the good things that you have done. Even though it was not what your teacher intended the assignment to be like, you helped a student: which at the end of the day is the most important part of being a teacher. Stop trying to please everyone, that will only cause you more stress. Do what you know how to do, what I know you are capable of. If you do this then soon everyone will be able to see your worth. Your stress and your fear are only temporary so there is no need to dwell on them. Focus on the good, focus on the experience, and learn and grow. You got this.
>
> Love,
> Your friend.
>
> P.S. you are going to be a fun teacher

Although the relationship with the cooperating teacher was a common source of stress for these preservice teachers, Sally offered herself self-compassion by encouraging herself not to let her one mistake doing things differently than her cooperating teacher "overshadow all the good things that [she had] done" to help support her students. Sally found a self-compassionate silver lining in her mistake when she noted that despite the mistake, she ultimately helped a student, which she believed "is the most important part of being a teacher." As mistakes are an inevitable part of being a person (Neff, 2011; Neff & Germer, 2018), responding to them with language that is imbued with self-compassion might encourage Sally to take more risks as she learns to become a teacher rather than to avoid mistakes (Johnston, 2003).

Anna demonstrated mindfulness by reminding herself that it's okay that "who" she was as a teacher was different from her cooperating teacher:

> First off, you are good enough. There is no question about it. You are smart, hard-working and compassionate. I know the next three semesters are going to be tough, but you will get through it and you will learn techniques that encourage engagement. Students now and your future students are going to love you because you genuinely care for them. This semester, focus on the classroom management strategies that you want to incorporate into your own classroom and those that do not align. Realize that [your cooperating teacher] has her own way of doing things with her students and they are

accustomed to how she operates the class. It is not a reflection of you as an aspiring educator.

Telling herself that she is "good enough . . . smart, hard-working and compassionate" helped Anna feel that the mismatch between her and her cooperating teacher's teaching styles was "not a reflection of" who she was "as an aspiring educator." Instead, she told herself that perhaps her students were just more "accustomed" to her cooperating teacher's methods.

Selena also wrote a self-compassionate letter about her relationship with her cooperating teacher:

> This week you are going to start your total teach. I know you've been worried about disappointing your CT [cooperating teacher] but you got it. The only person you need to work hard for is yourself. Your students love you, your CT loves you. They know you do everything with them in mind and now it's time to put that into use and use what you've learned to make these next 2 weeks great. This is what you've been working for and it's finally here. Make the best of it and don't stress yourself out! ASK QUESTIONS.

Here, Selena demonstrated a perceived positive relationship with her cooperating teacher, one that made her feel comfortable asking questions. As other researchers have found, a positive relationship with the cooperating teacher can reduce stress, particularly when the cooperating teacher seems to care about their social and emotional well-being (Murray-Harvey, 2000; Wetzel et al., 2017).

Write Your Own Self-Compassionate Letter That Addresses the Stress of Managing Relationship Dynamics With Cooperating Teachers

The self-compassion exercises I've written for you to respond to are aimed at addressing the stress you may be experiencing with your cooperating teacher, teacher educators, and your students' families. Like all the exercises in this book, they are adapted from a prompt by Neff (2011). I've also included some additional language in the exercise to address other potentially stressful relationship dynamics you may be experiencing as a new or developing teacher (e.g., other teachers, administrators, etc.). I want you to feel encouraged to adapt this exercise—and any of the self-compassion exercises within this book—to address the nuance of your particular situation and your needs. Role conflict is a very common challenge for preservice teachers. You are a student and a teacher at the same time, and you're working in someone else's classroom. Learning what your place is can be very stressful for you and your cooperating teacher. If you are having a hard time learning your place in your cooperating teacher's classroom, you aren't alone. Further, if there are parts of your identity that make your relationship with your cooperating teacher more challenging, you aren't alone either.

With this in mind, complete the following exercise (adapted from Neff, 2011), which will lead to you writing a self-compassionate letter about the stress of managing relationship dynamics with a cooperating teacher.

1. Consider this question: Do you have a classmate or colleague that you feel close to, either in your teacher education program or at your school? If yes, I want you to picture that person right now. If you don't have someone like that, it's ok; instead, imagine someone else in your life that you feel close to or imagine someone that you could feel close to.
2. Now, imagine that a best friend in your teacher education program (real or imaginary) is having the exact same struggle as you are learning their place in their cooperating teacher's classroom.
   » What would you say to them about this challenge?
   » Would you encourage them to communicate more openly with their cooperating teacher or seek out advice from a supportive teacher educator?
   » If this friend is noticing that part of the strain of this relationship may be connected to their identity, how would you address that with them in a compassionate way? Would you remind them that this is a challenge that many developing teachers experience? Or remind them that their cooperating teachers are also learning how to be mentors to student teachers?
   » How would you remind them to not be so hard on themselves about this challenging relationship?
3. Take some time to write your letter. Think about a time when you experienced stress due to managing a relationship dynamic with a cooperating teacher. Reflect on what you thought about *what you would say to your friend or colleague* in step 2 and how you would encourage them. Begin writing a letter to convey what you would tell them. However, instead of addressing the letter to the real or imagined friend, address it to yourself.

Stressful Relationships With Teacher Educators, Other Teachers, and Administrators. As the participants in my study expressed, these challenging relationship dynamics can also be present with their teacher educators. If you are struggling with an unsupportive teacher educator, is there a teacher educator you can identify that you can go to for advice? Can you talk with your fellow preservice teachers about coming together to discuss this challenge and feel less isolated? Could the act of coming together as a group perhaps inspire you to address these challenges with your teacher educator directly?

Other participants in this study expressed frustration when other teachers would step in and take over their attempts to address challenging student behavior. It made them feel that these other teachers did not believe they were capable of meeting their field students' needs (Barry, 2021). Are there other teachers in your grade-level team or school that make you feel bad about yourself as a new or developing teacher? If so, as the preservice teachers in this study described, you aren't alone. Is there someone on your grade-level team, perhaps your cooperating teacher or another friend or mentor, that you can lean on when dealing with this challenging relationship dynamic? What would you tell a dear friend having the exact same experience with a difficult colleague?

Finally, some of the preservice teachers in this study expressed being worried about how administrators perceived them (Barry, 2021). If you are a new or developing teacher, you may be experiencing similar challenges with demanding administrators (Dunn, 2018). If this is you, what would you say to a friend who was having an experience with a difficult or demanding administrator? Perhaps you feel they evaluated you unfairly or were unsupportive when you reached out for help. How would you encourage this friend to remember that everyone gets bad evaluations from time to time and that a single observation doesn't capture your worthiness as a teacher? If this administrator rejects your pleas for classroom materials or support with a challenging student, who can you reach out to for support? How would you remind this friend of the other supports they have in their professional community that they can reach out to if needed?

Example: My Self-Compassionate Letter About the Stress of Role Confusion With My Cooperating Teacher

I was very fortunate to have positive relationships with my colleagues and administrators when I became a teacher. Even as a preservice teacher, I remember several positive experiences with building administrators and my grade-level teams. I know from my own research that guides this book that this is not always the case (Barry, 2021), and I feel very fortunate to have had the support of colleagues and administrators in my field placements and in my own classroom.

That said, I had a few very painful experiences with unsupportive teacher educators as an undergraduate preservice teacher and as a doctoral student. I don't feel ready to share those just yet, so I've decided not to write about these experiences or offer you a self-compassionate letter addressing my challenges with my teacher educators (but I wrote plenty of them while I was in graduate school).

Although at first, I felt like not sharing them would mean I wasn't being open enough and that I wasn't delivering on the promise of this book, I now realize that keeping those things just for me and to draw clear boundaries was, in fact, an act of self-compassion. Similarly, you should not feel that anything you write about in these exercises belongs to anyone but you. Instead, I share what I hope will be a relatable self-compassionate letter in response to the challenging relationship dynamics I had while student teaching in pre-K.

> Dear Dave,
>
> It must have been really frustrating to have your cooperating teacher jump in and answer your questions when you were trying to give your pre-K students wait time. You have to remember that you were the first student teacher that she ever had, and that it's hard for teachers to share control of their classrooms, even though it was your takeover week. It was smart of you to share this with your field supervisor, because she was in a position that she could help you navigate that challenge. You have people around you that want to and can help you, you just need to remember to ask for help when you need it. I also want to remind you that other than this challenge in asserting your role in her classroom during your takeover week, you and your cooperating teacher had a really good relationship. She gave you a glowing recommendation when you were applying for jobs and was a great source of support. She was also a relatively new teacher who was still learning the skills needed to be a great teacher; adding you into the mix probably made that even more challenging. This experience will be good to remember when you work with preservice teachers and their cooperating teachers in the future.
>
> <3 Dave

Write Your Own Self-Compassionate Letter That Addresses the Stress of Managing Relationship Dynamics With Families

If you are a preservice teacher, you may not have had many opportunities to interact with your students' families yet. But don't worry, you will. The literature on challenges with families is somewhat sparse for preservice teachers, which is also reflected in the conversations I had with the preservice teachers in my study (Barry, 2021). It was something that preservice teachers appeared to know *will* be stressful from conversations with their cooperating teachers, rather than something they experienced firsthand; though as you read earlier, some did.

If you are a new or veteran teacher, you may think about the challenges of working with families a lot. When you have a classroom of your own and you are the sole teacher, all of the responsibilities that go along with being a teacher become yours. Teachers often report demanding and unrealistic parents and families as major sources of stress (Yong & Yue, 2007).

The Stress of Relationship Dynamics

If you are feeling worried about a challenging parent that you are currently working with or might work with in the future, consider the following exercise (adapted from Neff, 2011):

1. What words or phrases come to mind when you think about this challenging parent? What feelings does thinking about this parent or caregiver evoke in you? Do you believe that there are aspects of your identity that bring nuance to the challenges you're experiencing with this parent or family?
2. Now, imagine someone you care for deeply—real or imagined—expresses the exact same concern to you about a challenging parent.
    » What would you say to them?
    » How would you encourage them to be less self-critical and more self-kind?
    » How would you help them put things in perspective and remind them that many teachers express frustrations with families? If you have advice for this friend, what would it be?
3. Take some time to write your letter. Think about a time when you experienced stress due to managing a relationship dynamic with a student's parent. Reflect on what you thought about *what you would say to your friend or colleague* in step 2 and how you would encourage them. Begin writing a letter to convey what you would tell them. However, instead of addressing the letter to the real or imagined friend, address it to yourself.

Example: My Self-Compassionate Letter About the Stress of Managing Relationship Dynamics With Families

Dear Dave,

I'm so sorry that you felt that your students' families were criticizing your ability to be a teacher. It must be frustrating to feel that you are still learning how to be a teacher even though you are already a teacher, responsible for 22 kindergarteners all day every day. You want to "skip to the end" and be good at it already, but remember—becoming a good teacher takes time. With more time and experience, you're going to get better. As families get to know you, they're going to trust you more with their children. Being brand new, no one at the school—including your colleagues and administrators—can really speak to your teaching abilities yet. That could be scary for a parent bringing their child to school for the first time and having no information about what kind of teacher their child will have. They're entrusting the most important person in the world to them to a complete stranger with no track-record.

In most instances, the frustration you're feeling about parents stems from your already existing feelings of inadequacy and imposter syndrome. Looking back, it was really only one or two parents that first year that you felt were grilling you or were suspicious of you. The rest were so excited that their child had a male, guitar-playing, and creative teacher. With time, even those couple families you felt were critical of you came around and expressed how glad they were that you were their child's teacher. You started to get a wonderful reputation that first year and had very few problems with parents' trusting you moving forward, because they knew about you because of that wonderful reputation. Learning to navigate challenging relationships with families, just like learning to teach, is something that takes time and experience. Eventually, you got there, Dave!

CHAPTER 6

The Stress of Life Outside the Classroom

I have an incredible amount of empathy for the preservice teachers I work with who have jobs *in addition* to school and fieldwork now that I'm a teacher educator. I had three jobs on campus while I was student teaching to help fund my education. The job that took the most time was being the lead resident assistant (RA) for the office of residence life. Not only was I responsible for the residents on my floor, I was responsible for mentoring the other RAs who were learning the job. I also had to organize programming for the residents of the dorm and help the other RAs in planning and executing theirs. I met with each of them weekly on top of making our schedules for who would be "on duty" in the building each day if any issues arose with our residents. Being "on duty" meant doing rounds through the building and being available when students were locked out of their rooms or needed anything.

We were technically on duty until the next morning, so we would need to respond if anything happened overnight. I'd be sitting in my dorm room working on lesson plans and be interrupted at least once every 30 minutes by a resident who was locked out or who was having a conflict with their roommate. When I wasn't there, I was working as a short-order cook in the freshman dorm cafeteria to pay for gas to get to and from student teaching and the occasional dinner out with my friends. I was also the TA (teaching assistant) for an introductory piano course and would meet with students to help them learn to read music and the basic techniques of piano (which is where my piano skills started and ended).

> I was incredibly stressed out about money in college because I didn't have any. I didn't get paid to be an RA, but it covered the cost of my room and board, which meant I wouldn't need to take out quite as many loans. I had to maintain a certain GPA to keep my scholarships, which I managed to do despite having very little time each day to study and work on my assignments.

> I was also a college student and wanted to spend as much time with my friends as possible, which often meant going to see them really late at night when I was done with work and my homework—as long as I wasn't on duty. I'd miss out on the sleep I would need to be on my A-game at student teaching the next morning, and the stress and lack of sleep resulted in me developing an eye twitch and getting no fewer than three sties in my eye during the student teaching semester. They were, without fail, all huge sties that would inflate my eyelid to the point where it looked like I was having an allergic reaction in one eye. They hurt, looked terrible, and made me worry that I would scare the children I was working with as a student teacher.
>
> Applying for jobs and going on job interviews became a fourth job on top of class and student teaching. Having gotten my driver's license so that I could student teach at 22 years old, I was driving into Boston with no idea where I was going, and GPS was not a thing yet. I would tape printed copies of MapQuest directions to my steering wheel and highlight the "really important" parts, but if you've every driven in Boston, you know that there's no preparing you for how scary and complicated it is—especially for a new driver! I didn't write about many of these challenges in my student teaching journal, as they weren't specifically connected to the work I was doing with students. That said, being stretched so thin and being so stressed about money and time management of course impacted my ability to be my best in the classroom every day.

WHY IS BALANCING LIFE OUTSIDE THE CLASSROOM STRESSFUL FOR PRESERVICE TEACHERS?

Maggie, one of the cohort coordinators in this teacher education program, described how she attempted to be consistent and supportive by reiterating she was "there to support and guide" the preservice teachers as they navigated all of the different stressors associated within and outside of the teacher education program. In our interview, she said:

> We need to keep reiterating throughout the semesters we have them that we are there to support them and guide them. And, and there's times that things are very tricky. I've had some [preservice teachers] say "I'm going to drop out" and I say "how can I help you not to drop out?"

For Maggie, it seemed that hearing the concerns that had led some preservice teachers to want to "drop out" of the teacher education program and then offering to help in substantive ways was one way she aimed to support the preservice teachers who were feeling overwhelmed.

Rose, a field supervisor who worked with Maggie, explained ways that Maggie attempted to follow through with this kind of tangible support:

I've talked with Maggie about bringing in some people from the counseling center to talk about managing stress and things like that. And so maybe giving those extra supports to help the PSTs [preservice teachers] figure out, especially from the beginning, how to kind of balance it all because it really is a balancing act. Having those tools to help them from the get-go could be really beneficial.

From Rose's perspective, one way that she (a field supervisor) and Maggie (a cohort coordinator) could support preservice teachers manage the "balancing act" required of them was to find ways to provide them with actionable support (e.g., "bring in some people from the counseling center"). This aligns with the kind of support the preservice teachers said they needed but were not receiving from their course instructors and professors (Barry, 2021).

Preservice Teachers With Jobs

One of the challenges these preservice teachers experienced resonated with me deeply: needing to have a job in addition to being a full-time student and preservice teacher. For example, Anna, who put herself through the teacher education program by working at a local restaurant described how she felt the program was not designed with all students in mind, particularly students who had responsibilities (i.e., work) outside of class and field. In our second interview, when she was a first-year teacher, Anna said:

> I think that ultimately the [teacher education program] is for students who do not have other responsibilities other than going to class and being in the classroom. I don't think the program is necessarily for students who have jobs, or who have families, or who have other responsibilities. I think that's really sad.

Anna was describing the challenges some preservice teachers experience in relation to time commitments outside of courses and fieldwork that make balancing those commitments stressful (Horgan et al., 2018; Zimmerman et al., 2008). From her perspective, this teacher education program was not designed for students who had such commitments. Rose, a field supervisor, also described how needing to work presented challenges for preservice teachers:

> A lot of them also work. And so balancing work on top of fieldwork and a lot of courses can be quite difficult. I experienced that in another cohort that I work with as well. They find it hard to find that balance.

Although the teacher education program would become less overwhelming for some preservice teachers as time went on (Barry, 2021), which aligns with previous research (Murray-Harvey et al., 2000), this was not the case for students who had jobs, which, according to Rose, "a lot of them" had. Finally, Maggie, a cohort coordinator, described how despite the challenges of needing to work to pay tuition, many of the preservice teachers she had worked with over the years "persevered":

> I've got my students that work many hours to make it. Or those that don't have enough money for tuition. You know, they're amazing students and you know they're going to do well, but that always becomes something that you notice with those that have financial support and those that don't. And I'm not saying they don't do as well, because some of those that really, really work hard, they persevere and they're, you know, they're just tenacious throughout those 3 semesters and you know they're going to do well.

Although Maggie described the students who needed to work experiencing additional challenges in ways similar to Anna and Rose, she believed that many students who had these additional challenges were more than capable of taking them on and were ultimately successful in the teacher education program.

ADDRESSING THE STRESS OF LIFE OUTSIDE THE CLASSROOM WITH SELF-COMPASSION

Some preservice teachers demonstrated self-compassion when they wrote self-compassionate letters that identified the specific barrier that might have been preventing them from feeling successful when it came to balancing their lives with the teacher education program.

Excerpts From Educators' Self-Compassionate Letters

In some instances, the preservice teachers offered themselves a plan to address these external stressors rather than be overwhelmed by them. For example, Cara wrote:

> Dear Cara,
>
> Hey girl, I know you have been having a hard time. Everything will be better soon, you just have to get through the next few weeks. After that you will be done with your first semester in the [teacher education program]. Also, I know it might be hard to hear, and I only want the best for you when I say this: Maybe you should schedule some time for homework: have Friday from 5–8 be homework time. You are so loved and it makes me feel really bad to see you so sad/sick/stressed. The three "S's"! Yikes. I love you. Everything will be ok.

In this letter, Cara acknowledged she has "been having a hard time," but instead of judging herself, she gave herself a plan to get her homework done.

Still others demonstrated self-compassion by reminding themselves of who they believed they "were" and that their challenges or failures did not define them. Like Cara, Aria did this while simultaneously reminding herself how loved she is by others:

> Aria,
>
> You are okay. Everything is going to be okay. Life might seem stressful or overwhelming right now but you have to roll with the punches. You are stronger than you believe you are. I know you're scared you'll never become what you want to be or find your true passion but you will. Life is a process. You are so young. You have so much life ahead of you to figure stuff out. You've always wished you just knew what you were called to do—but it's okay if you don't yet. You are so loved. So accepted. And so passionate about so many different things. Stop beating yourself up about not knowing. Not knowing is half of the fun. Embrace that. And know that you can still be anything you want to be. It's not too late to start over. It's really never too late. But life isn't going to make itself happen—you have to do that on your own. Be persistent. And mostly—never give up.

Aria demonstrated self-compassion in this letter by reminding herself that it is ok not to know what the future will hold—in fact, it is not possible to know what the future will hold—and that "beating yourself up about not knowing" is something she should stop doing (Siegel, 2010).

Cara used similar loving language in another one of her self-compassionate letters:

> Dear Cara,
>
> Hey babe, I know it's been kind of stressful over the past two weeks. Most of the reasons have been out of your control. But the ones that aren't we should try to work on. I know you have been waking up later because you have been helping [a friend], but you also need to work on you. It's okay that you have been struggling but you—we—can do better.

Cara's letter was imbued with self-kindness because she encouraged herself to take better care of herself—that she "need[s] to work on" herself. Furthermore, her letter counters critiques of self-compassion that mistake self-compassion for self-centeredness or self-indulgence (Germer & Neff, 2017; Neff, 2011; Neff & Germer, 2018). Instead, Cara acknowledged her struggle and her need to "work on" what is within her control and her belief that she "can do better."

Quinn, who was excluded from graduation exercises because of a credit she was required to make up (and made it up that summer), wrote herself this self-compassionate letter that emphasized that despite being excluded, she was still deserving of self-compassion:

Dear self,

Just because you may not be able to be included in a ceremony does not negate all of the work you have done thus far. You have worked so hard to get where you are today. You have changed so much this past year. You will never be perfect, but you are ready, strengths and weaknesses included. Good luck.

You may remember from the previous chapters that Quinn experienced additional challenges during her time in the teacher education program (e.g., not feeling supported by her cooperating teacher) but demonstrated in this letter that despite those challenges, she remained encouraged by her progress and hard work. In this way, Quinn seemed to offer herself these words with a heightened capacity to acknowledge her growth and keep going rather than be overwhelmed by a perceived failure; just as a good friend would encourage her to do (Neff, 2011; Neff & Germer, 2018).

Finally, Cara encouraged herself to seek support from others in one of her final self-compassionate letters:

Dear Cara,

It's here. Student teaching. The final semester. It won't be as hard. Honestly, I feel this is going to be your best semester yet. Not as much work and you have a plan. Contact the mental health center. Start before the big changes start again. You'll do great.

—Cara

Across all of these examples, a common realization for these preservice teachers was that one way to manage their experiences with stress in and outside the teacher education program was to seek help from others—their cooperating teachers, friends and fellow preservice teachers, and mental health professionals. They offer themselves compassion for needing help through these letters, which may be read as encouraging connectivity to people who can support them. In this way, that encouragement is self-compassionate because it is encouragement to pursue connection, or common humanity (Neff, 2011; Neff & Germer, 2018).

Write Your Own Self-Compassionate Letter That Addresses the Stress of Balancing Life Outside the Classroom

You are so much more than a student, a preservice teacher, or a developing teacher. It would be incredible if your student teaching experience or your first year of teaching could be solely focused on learning to be a teacher, but that's just not how life works. Nothing happens in a vacuum, and life will throw us curveballs we can't anticipate. We can't eliminate the stress we feel when we need to hold additional jobs, when we try to have a social life, and when needing to make rent every month. With all of this in mind, consider the following exercise based on Neff's "Exploring Self-Compassion Through Letter Writing" (2011).

1. What words or phrases come to mind when you think about the challenges that exist outside of your classroom or teacher education program? In what ways might certain aspects of your identity bring nuance to these additional challenges? More importantly, how do these challenges make you feel about yourself as a person—not just a teacher?
2. Consider this question: Do you have a classmate or colleague that you feel close to, either in your teacher education program or at your school? If yes, I want you to picture that person right now. If you don't have someone like that, it's ok; instead, imagine someone else in your life that you feel close to or imagine someone that you could feel close to.
3. Now imagine that a dear friend—real or imagined—was experiencing the same challenges in their life while they were also learning to become a teacher.
    » What would you say to them about these challenges?
    » How would you remind them that learning to be a teacher is already hard and that having to deal with additional challenges in their personal lives would be hard for any new or developing teacher?
    » If this friend were to feel that there were certain aspects of their identity that brought nuance to these challenges, how would you encourage them?
4. Take some time to write your letter. Think about a time when you experienced stress due to balancing life outside the classroom. Reflect on what you thought about *what you would say to your friend or colleague* in step 3 and how you would encourage them. Begin writing a letter to convey what you would tell them. However, instead of addressing the letter to the real or imagined friend, address it to yourself.

Example: My Experience Balancing Three Jobs and Student Teaching and a Social Life

Dear Dave,

As I read over the challenges you experienced while you were learning to become a teacher, a few things come to mind. First, I am so proud that you were able to get through your teacher education program when you were also working so you could pay for college. That wasn't something many of your classmates needed to do, and it was a lot. I wish that you hadn't needed to work so you could've put all of your efforts into learning to be a teacher, but somehow, you still managed to put an incredible amount of yourself into your student teaching experience. You got great feedback from your cooperating teachers and field supervisor despite the fact that you were burning yourself out.

And then, when you graduated, you not only had to learn how to manage everything about being a teacher, you had to learn how to be an independent adult. Managing your bills, trying to see friends whenever you could, traveling for a long-distance relationship—it was all a lot to suddenly be responsible for. This is something that most people go through when they graduate college and start jobs—learning how to be completely independent. Despite the credit card debt and the occasional month where you weren't sure you'd be able to keep the lights on, you made it through and it got easier. Like learning to be a teacher—or any new skill—figuring out who you are on your own and how to be independent takes time and mistakes. You were able to learn from these challenges and become more confident in yourself as an independent adult, which you should be proud of.

You often expressed worry about being the only male in your teacher education program and then being the only male kindergarten teacher at your school. There were several times that you felt people were suspicious of your intentions for wanting to be a kindergarten teacher, even though it had been your lifelong dream. Being gay made this more complicated. We are still living in a time where people are legally allowed to discriminate against you because of your sexuality, which is horrible and unfair. With bigoted people targeting queer representation in children's literature and the direct impact that has on a classroom library, it is no wonder that you felt that you had to keep who you are hidden from your students' families. In retrospect, I think many of them knew, but it was just one of those things that never got talked about. I'm so sorry you didn't feel safe expressing your full self in the way it seemed others could. I truly believe that the anti-LGBTQIA+ rhetoric that has resurfaced recently is no more than the homophobic rantings of a few hate groups that are just loud. The majority of Americans believe that you and other members of the LGBTQIA+ community deserve the same rights and respect as everyone else and are working hard every day to ensure that you and your community have the same rights as everyone else. I know this feels like an omnipresent tension, but smart and organized people are on your side and ready to defend your personhood. Don't be afraid of who you are, and lean on those who are able to stand up for you when you're too tired to stand up for yourself. But keep getting up when life throws you punches and never be ashamed of who you are.

Love,
Dave

CHAPTER 7

Moving Forward With Self-Compassion
A Call for Stakeholders to Take Action

As a former Boston Public School kindergarten teacher, I began this work keenly aware of how stress and burnout impact teachers as a result of my own experiences with stress and burnout (Chang, 2009; Maslach & Leiter, 2016; Ryan et al., 2017). Reading these former preservice teachers' fieldwork journals and listening to them speak about their experiences with stressors, challenges, and feelings of inadequacy in their teacher education program brought up a lot of memories for me from my own teaching and preservice teaching experiences. Reading their self-compassionate letters made me wish I had been given the opportunity to address these challenges in the ways they did. If I were to go back and do my preservice teacher education again, I hope I would encourage myself to keep trying, to see my mistakes as learning opportunities, and to find self-compassionate silver linings in the challenges I faced as a new and developing teacher.

A vivid memory of my cooperating teacher "snapping" at me (as Quinn described) for allowing a child to go to the bathroom at "the wrong time" (as Nora described) came flooding back when reviewing their letters. I remember that after being yelled at by my cooperating teacher, I pretended I needed to use the bathroom (as I later learned the particular 2nd-grade child I allowed to go to the bathroom was known to do) to go into the staff bathroom and cry; I had not thought about that experience in years.

It was a deeply emotional experience reading their journals and hearing them discuss the challenges they experienced, but not only because so many of their experiences mirrored and triggered my own. As I went through the data, I felt simultaneously sad for them and angry that not much has changed in these feelings among preservice teachers and how little has been done to address these common feelings of stress that have been found by researchers and teacher educators (Beltman et al., 2011; Hirshberg, 2017; Horgan et al., 2018).

However, I also found myself feeling hopeful. As higher levels of self-compassion are associated with high levels of job satisfaction and fewer instances of burnout among professional caregivers (Barnard & Curry, 2012; Delaney, 2018; Duarte et al., 2016; Eriksson et al., 2018; Finlay-Jones et al., 2015; Knier et al., 2020; Neff et al., 2020; Stebnicki, 2015; Yela et al., 2019) and participation in the Mindful Self-Compassion Program has been shown to increase self-compassion (Neff & Germer, 2018), a self-compassion exercise seemed to be an appropriate way to address these challenges among preservice teachers.

As for the preservice teachers in my study, they did in fact experience a statistically significant increase in their ratings of self-compassion over time, which, as explained in Chapter 2, they credit to the opportunity to practice self-compassion throughout their enrollment in their teacher education program. The hope I have found here is that you, my reader, can now understand the benefits of practicing self-compassion for early childhood teachers and preservice teachers (Barry, 2021, 2022, 2023). Moreover, I hope that you'll continue to revisit the prompts and letters that I and the preservice teachers in my study shared throughout and that you'll continue to practice self-compassion. Furthermore, I hope as you continue this practice that you evaluate your self-compassion score periodically to see how you may be becoming more self-compassionate over time—you deserve it. You can find Neff's Self-Compassion Scale: Short Form (Raes et al., 2011) in Appendix A.

SCHOLARLY SIGNIFICANCE OF SELF-COMPASSIONATE LETTER-WRITING WITH PRESERVICE TEACHERS

There are not many studies that address preservice teachers' stress (Beltman et al., 2010; Hirshberg, 2017), and to date there is limited knowledge about whether particular elements of the Mindful Self-Compassion (MSC) Program could successfully address their experiences with stress (of which self-compassionate letter writing exercise is one). Furthermore, I was not able to find any studies in which the self-compassionate letters written as part of the Mindful Self-Compassion Program were collected and analyzed as data, although a few studies have evaluated the utility of self-compassionate writing using different prompts with mixed results (Dreisoerner et al., 2020; Wong & Mak, 2016). Finally, there are few studies that evaluate the impact of participating in exercises from the MSC among women of color (Finlay-Jones et al., 2017; Wong & Mak, 2016; Yarnell et al., 2015). Taken together, this work sheds new light on how a diverse cohort of preservice teachers approached participating in a particular exercise from the MSC Program. However, the responsibility of a preservice teacher's stress cannot rest solely on their own shoulders.

IMPLICATIONS FOR EARLY CHILDHOOD STAKEHOLDERS

Researchers have found that teachers' experiences with stress are being linked to burnout and turnover (Dunn, 2018; Ryan et al., 2017), that teacher turnover has a negative impact on student achievement (Fantilli & McDougall, 2009), and that teacher turnover disproportionately impacts children of color in low-income, racially segregated school districts (Djonko-Moore, 2016). This is even more pronounced post-pandemic, with attrition rates in these communities reaching 12–14% (Diliberti & Schwartz, 2023). Therefore, many stakeholders, policymakers in particular, should have a vested interest in mitigating teachers' experiences with stress early and often, particularly because a teacher's stress management strategies—whether positive or negative—typically begin during their preservice teacher education (Gold, 1985; Horgan et al., 2018).

Policymakers

While practicing self-compassion seems to have supported and eased the impact of stress experienced by these preservice teachers, serious changes need to be made at a policy level to mitigate these stressors. Meaning, self-compassion should not be considered a Band-aid for stressors that need not exist within teacher educations programs when there are ways policymakers can take steps to reduce feelings of stress among preservice teachers and address burnout among teachers. Some ideas for how policymakers could do this are shared next.

The fact that some preservice teachers need to work in order to put themselves through college on top of their coursework and field placements disregards what is known about preservice teachers' stress, despite how limited that scholarship is (Beltman et al., 2010; Dunn, 2018; Gold, 1985). For that reason, policymakers should provide greater financial support to teacher education programs so that preservice teachers have access to need-based scholarships and grants and priority access to student jobs that reduce tuition. To do so would lessen the financial burden of attending teacher education programs and becoming a teacher.

As researchers have found, teachers are incredibly stressed (Adams, 2013; Dunn, 2018; Ryan et al., 2017; Simos, 2013; Yong & Yue, 2007); to add an additional responsibility (i.e., a student teacher) without some sort of compensation disregards that stress. One opportunity to incentivize cooperating teachers to take on mentoring roles with preservice teachers could come in the form of vouchers for graduate courses at the college or university at which their preservice teacher is enrolled. As many public school teachers are compensated more for graduate credits they earn (as I was in the Boston Public Schools), this is one way that policymakers could assist teacher education programs in supporting the cooperating teachers their preservice teachers work with—by providing them with ways to be paid more at work and to continue to develop their own knowledge and practice as teachers. I am unaware if this is still the case, but while I was teaching in Boston, there were certain teacher education programs that would offer such vouchers to cooperating teachers that, when accumulated, would increase that teacher's total number of graduate credits and, ultimately, their pay grade.

Teacher Educators

Teacher educators could support each other in this process by collaborating on shared policies for addressing in their coursework and teaching methods what the preservice teachers in this study described needing, including more deliberate links between the theoretical and the practical (Onchwari, 2010). Similarly, teacher educators should study and expand the small canon of research about the stress preservice teachers experience in order to plan their syllabi, course sequences, late work policies, and so on in ways that are more attentive to the challenges and stressors preservice teachers experience. Having teacher educators who are aware of and account for these challenges might bring about more empathy for the stress researchers have found abounds among preservice teachers (e.g., Horgan et al., 2018). Additionally, teacher educators could appear more empathetic by sharing stories with the preservice teachers in their courses about their own mistakes and missteps from when they were new and developing teachers and what they learned from these experiences.

Thoughtfully Matching Preservice Teachers With Cooperating Teachers. This study and other researchers have found that the relationship between cooperating teachers and preservice teachers impacts the latter's experience with stress, for better or for worse (Barry, 2021; Murray-Harvey et al., 2000). As you read throughout this book, every preservice teacher is different and inevitably has different needs and challenges; as you read, how their cooperating teachers responded to those needs and challenges varied. Therefore, there are reasons for teacher educators to take serious measures when matching their preservice teachers with cooperating teachers. Doing so could ensure a positive relationship that supports preservice teachers with the technical (Costa et al., 2016) and emotional (Wetzel et al., 2017) aspects of learning to become teachers. For example, each preservice teacher and cooperating teacher could fill out a survey before they are matched in which each cooperating teacher indicates their coaching and support style, as well as their boundaries about what many of these preservice teachers described as "stepping on their toes" as they learned to assert themselves as teachers. Each preservice teacher could also indicate the kind of support they believe they need. These surveys could then be used to match them accordingly based on style, strengths, and needs.

Creating Access to Counselors. Teacher educators should also address the stress preservice teachers are experiencing by providing them with access to a neutral, confidential support system such as those from a counseling center, as Maggie (one of the cohort coordinators) and Rose (one of the field supervisors) attempted. As these preservice teachers expressed that venting to each other was helpful but that they had concerns about venting to their teacher educators for fear of retaliation (e.g., Alycia), having a neutral person (e.g., a counselor) who could lead groups of preservice teachers in discussions about their stress might be helpful. This could be particularly useful when they experience challenges with specific teacher educators and cooperating teachers. That said, time is a concern for preservice teachers (Horgan et al., 2018; Zimmerman et al., 2008), and scheduling these venting sessions may make accessing them challenging. One way teacher educators could demonstrate their commitment to this need would be to make time for these sessions during a monthly seminar or class session. Giving up instructional time in their courses would be another way that teacher educators could take action in regard to their commitment to the well-being of their preservice teachers.

An additional benefit to providing access to a neutral counselor would be the potential opportunities for preservice teachers to feel more connected to their peers. By learning that their peers are also experiencing challenges and by supporting them, preservice teachers could also develop self-compassion in such a setting by way of common humanity (Neff, 2011).

Making Space for Self-Compassion. An additional implication of this work came from interviews with the preservice teachers who felt that prioritizing self-compassion should happen in more than just the first 10 minutes of their seminars (e.g., Nicole, Maria, Quinn). As Nicole said:

> I feel like that honestly [self-compassion] should be the lead way into the TEP [teacher education program] because if you're not spending the time to help yourself to make sure you're in a good place, I don't think you'll be prepared to help somebody else be in a good place, especially children. So for me, I think that needs to be the lead way. For sure.

One way in which Nicole's sentiment could be implicated would be for the teacher educators to make slight tweaks to their coursework to prioritize self-compassion practice within their coursework like Nana did. Nana said:

> I think it was a very useful exercise. In fact, I've kept that as my journal piece. "I felt successful when and I felt unsuccessful when." Every person is individualized.

As a teacher educator, I have designed and implemented a practice in my own courses that I call "7 for the self" (Brown et al., 2020). My colleagues and I described this practice in an article:

> Rather than reminding PSTs [preservice teachers] in this course to take care of themselves on their own time, which is limited for PSTs (Horgan et al., 2018), the second author [i.e., me] offers the first 7 minutes of class for students to engage in whatever self-care activity "works best" for them (e.g. make phone calls, chat with a classmate, journal, etc.). pp. 264–265

In this way, we suggested that there are opportunities within coursework to prioritize preservice teachers' well-being.

CONCLUDING THOUGHTS

If new and developing early childhood teachers are able to stay in their classrooms healthfully and sustainably, developing self-compassion among teachers also holds promise for student achievement, for as researchers have found, experienced teachers have the greatest impact on student success (Darling-Hammond, 2000; Fantilli & McDougall, 2009). Furthermore, these former preservice teachers believe they respond more mindfully (i.e., less punitively) to challenging situations with students after participating in this self-compassionate letter-writing exercise within and across their 3-semester teacher education program. Taken together, access to an experienced and self-compassionate teacher holds promise for more equitable learning experiences for children who have historically been marginalized in schools. For all these reasons, the time to address new and developing early childhood teachers' stress is now, and to do so with self-compassion is one way to do this.

APPENDIX A

Self-Compassion Scale—Short Form (SCS-SF) (Raes et al., 2011)

HOW I TYPICALLY ACT TOWARDS MYSELF IN DIFFICULT TIMES

Please read each statement carefully before answering. To the left of each item, indicate how often you behave in the stated manner, using the following scale:

Almost never				Almost always
1	2	3	4	5

1. When I fail at something important to me, I become consumed by feelings of inadequacy.
2. I try to be understanding and patient towards those aspects of my personality I don't like.
3. When something painful happens, I try to take a balanced view of the situation.
4. When I'm feeling down, I tend to feel like most other people are probably happier than I am.
5. I try to see my failings as part of the human condition.
6. When I'm going through a very hard time, I give myself the caring and tenderness I need.
7. When something upsets me, I try to keep my emotions in balance.
8. When I fail at something that's important to me, I tend to feel alone in my failure.
9. When I'm feeling down, I tend to obsess and fixate on everything that's wrong.
10. When I feel inadequate in some way, I try to remind myself that feelings of inadequacy are shared by most people.
11. I'm disapproving and judgmental about my own flaws and inadequacies.
12. I'm intolerant and impatient towards those aspects of my personality I don't like.

Self-Compassion Scale–Short Form (SCS-SF) (Raes et al., 2011)

Coding Key:

Self-Kindness Items: 2, 6
Self-Judgment Items: 11, 12
Common Humanity Items: 5, 10
Isolation Items: 4, 8
Mindfulness Items: 3, 7
Over-identified Items: 1, 9

Subscale scores are computed by calculating the mean of subscale item responses. To compute a total self-compassion score, reverse score the negative subscale items—self-judgment, isolation, and over-identification (i.e., $1=5$, $2=4$, $3=3$, $4=2$, $5=1$)—then compute a total mean.

APPENDIX B

Participant Information and Statistical Tests

Table B.1: Descriptive Statistics of Self-Compassion Scale

Pseudonyms	TEP role	Participant Identity Statement from Interview	Int. 1	Int. 2	SCL	J1	J2	J3	SC 1	SC 2	SC 3
*Alycia	PST	"Female, Hispanic, Catholic, family oriented"	X		9	X	X	X	3.75	3.58	3.67
*Amy	PST	"White female"	X	X	9	X	X	X	2.58		2.5
*Anna	PST	"Anglo-American female"	X	X	9	X	X		3.5	3.75	3.92
*Bob	PST	"I think of myself as half Asian, half White and then culturally, half Korean, half American; and female and Catholic."	X	X	11	X	X	X			
*Elaine	PST	"African American woman; I'm Christian."	X	X	9	X	X	X	3.5	3.58	4.08
*Leslie	PST	"Hispanic, female, and Christian"	X	X	10	X	X	X	3.66	3.83	3.83

(*continued*)

Table B.1 (continued)

Pseudonyms	TEP role	Participant Identity Statement from Interview	Int. 1	Int. 2	SCL	J1	J2	J3	SC 1	SC 2	SC 3
*Maria	PST	"I feel like the way that I explore my identity the most is through a lot of my artwork and through images . . . but if I have to make the more socially acceptable statement, female, Latina, Mexican American, liberal."	X	X	8	X	X	X			4.42
*Nicole	PST	"Female and culturally mixed. I'm half Lebanese, half German-Irish. I tend to follow my father's religion, which is Islam; I'm open-minded."	X	X	11	X		X	2.58	3.25	4.42
*Quinn	PST	"Cis-gender White woman"	X	X	9	X	X	X	1.42	2.25	2.33
*Selena	PST	"Latina; second-generation"	X	X	7	X	X	X	2.75	2.92	3.08
Alice	PST				9	X	X		2.08	2.25	2.33
Cara	PST				8	X	X	X	3.75	3.33	3.67
Nora	PST				6	X	X	X		3.17	2.92
Sally	PST				11	X	X	X	2.75		3.58
Sophia	PST				5	X	X	X	2.33	2.75	3.17
Tamara	PST				11	X	X	X	4.67	4.33	4.25

Pseudonyms	TEP role	Participant Identity Statement from Interview	Int. 1	Int. 2	SCL	J1	J2	J3	SC 1	SC 2	SC 3
*Maggie	CC	"Assistant Professor of Practice"; "I'm always a teacher at heart"; former administrator, "I was an ESL reading specialist."	X								
*Nana	CC	"I started my journey as an educator teaching special education"; "I became a special ed instructional coordinator"; "I got assigned to be an assistant principal"; ultimately became principal in TEP area.	X								
*Alex	FS	"I grew up in the DMV area"; "I'm really passionate about black girls and their experiences at school"; "I was a teacher before this"; "Black, gay woman."	X								

(*continued*)

Table B.1 (continued)

Pseudonyms	TEP role	Participant Identity Statement from Interview	Int. 1	Int. 2	SCL	J1	J2	J3	SC 1	SC 2	SC 3
*Clare	FS	"I identify as a White woman. I have also worked with undergrads for many years because I was a lab school teacher."	X								
*Elizabeth	FS	"White female grew up in the area, so familiar with [this city and TEP]"; "I am coming from like the physical education world."	X								
*Rose	FS	"I'm a white female in her mid-twenties . . . originally from the Midwest"; "former teacher"; "working on my PhD now."	X								
*Susan	FS	"I'll call myself a middle-aged White woman who has taught for 19 years"; "mostly I've taught childhood"; "I was a cooperating teacher for [this TEP]."	X								

KEY

*pseudonym chosen by participant
TEP = Teacher Education Program
PST = Preservice Teacher
CC = Cohort Coordinator
FS = Field Supervisor
Int. 1 = Interview 1
Int. 2 = follow-up interview
SCL = Total Self-Compassionate Letters written by participant
J1, J2, J3 = journal 1, 2, 3
SC 1,2,3 = Self-Compassion scores 1,2,3

Descriptive Statistics

	N	Minimum	Maximum	Mean	Std. Deviation
scale 1	14	1.42	4.67	2.9457	.88770
scale 2	13	2.25	4.33	3.2746	.60850
scale 3	16	2.33	4.42	3.5369	.66945
Valid N (listwise)	12				

Table B.2: Paired Sample T-Tests of Self-Compassion Scale

Paired Samples Test of Preservice Teachers' Mean Self-Compassion Scores (Semester 1, 2, & 3)

	Compared Semesters (1, 2, & 3)	Paired Differences							
		Mean	Std. Deviation	Std. Error Mean	95% Confidence		t	df	Sig. (2-tailed)
					Lower	Upper			
Pair 1	Semester 1–Semester 2	-0.29083	0.56659	0.16356	-0.65083	0.06916	-1.778	11	0.103
Pair 2	Semester 2–Semester 3	-0.27077	0.35615	0.09878	-0.48599	-0.05555	-2.741	12	0.018
Pair 3	Semester 1–Semester 3	-0.57214	0.74427	0.19892	-1.00187	-0.14241	-2.876	13	0.013

Paired Samples Effect Sizes of Preservice Teachers' Mean Self-Compassion Scores (Semester

	Compared Semesters (1, 2, & 3)		Standardizer[a]	Point Estimate (Cohen's d effect size)	95% Confidence	
					Lower	Upper
Pair 1	Semester 1–Semester 2	Cohen's d	0.56659	-0.513	-1.107	0.101
Pair 2	Semester 2–Semester 3	Cohen's d	0.35615	-0.760	-1.370	-0.127
Pair 3	Semester 1–Semester 3	Cohen's d	0.74427	-0.769	-1.358	-0.158

[a] The denominator used in estimating the effect sizes.

Cohen's d uses the sample standard deviation of the mean difference.

(Barry, 2021; 2023)

References

Abenavoli, R. M., Jennings, P. A., Greenberg, M. T., Harris, A. R., & Katz, D. A. (2013). The protective effects of mindfulness against burnout among educators. *Psychology of Education Review, 37*(2), 13.

Achinstein, B., Ogawa, R. T., Sexton, D., & Freitas, C. (2010). Retaining teachers of color: A pressing problem and a potential strategy for "hard-to-staff" schools. *Review of Educational Research, 80*(1), 71–107.

Adams, R. (2013, May 1). Headteacher killed herself after six months in job, coroner rules. *The Guardian.* https://www.theguardian.com/education/2013/may/01/headteacher-kills-herself

Amos, Y. T. (2010). "They don't want to get it!" Interaction between minority and White pre-service teachers in a multicultural education class. *Multicultural Education, 17*(4), 31–37.

Amrani, P. (2010). *Loving-kindness: Self-compassion, burnout and empathy among therapists* [Doctoral dissertation]. UMI. (3420446)

Barnard, L. K., & Curry, J. F. (2012). The relationship of clergy burnout to self-compassion and other personality dimensions. *Pastoral Psychology, 61*(2), 149–163.

Barry, D. P. (2021). *Self-compassionate letter writing as a potential way to mitigate feelings of stress, empathy fatigue, and burnout among preservice teachers* [Unpublished doctoral dissertation]. University of Texas at Austin.

Barry, D. P. (2022, November). *Developing a self-compassionate growth mindset about teaching young children* [Conference session]. NAECTE Conference, Washington, DC.

Barry, D. P. (2023). Self-compassion practice to mitigate teachers' empathy fatigue and burnout. In O. Schepers, M. Brennan, & P. Bernhardt (Eds.), *Developing trauma-informed teachers: Creating classrooms that foster equity, resiliency, and asset-based approaches: Research findings from the field* (pp. 49–70). Information Age Publishing.

Beltman, S., Mansfield, C., & Price, A. (2011). Thriving not just surviving: A review of research on teacher resilience. *Educational Research Review, 6*(3), 185–207.

Benzo, R. P., Kirsch, J. L., & Nelson, C. (2017). Compassion, mindfulness, and the happiness of healthcare workers. *Explore, 13*(3), 201–206.

Beshai, S., McAlpine, L., Weare, K., & Kuyken, W. (2016). A non-randomised feasibility trial assessing the efficacy of a mindfulness-based intervention for teachers to reduce stress and improve well-being. *Mindfulness, 7*(1), 198–208.

Bishop, S. R., Lau, M., Shapiro, S. L., Carlson, L. E., Anderson, N. D., Carmody, J., Segal, Z., Abbey, S., Speca, M., Velting, D., & Devins, G. (2004). Mindfulness:

A proposed operational definition. *Clinical Psychology: Science and Practice, 11*(3), 230–241.

Borko, H., & Cadwell, J. (1982). Individual differences in teachers' decision strategies: An investigation of classroom organization and management decisions. *Journal of Educational Psychology, 74*(4), 598–610.

Brown, C. P., Barry, D. P., Ku, D., & Puckett, K. (2020). Teach as I say, not as I do: How preservice teachers made sense of the mismatch between how they were expected to teach and how they were taught in their professional training program. *The Teacher Educator, 56*(3), 250–269.

Cannon, W. B. (1932). *The wisdom of the body*. W. W. Norton.

Carrillo, J. (2010). Teaching that breaks your heart: Reflections on the soul wounds of a first-year Latina teacher. *Harvard Educational Review, 80*(1), 74–81.

Chang, M. L. (2009). An appraisal perspective of teacher burnout: Examining the emotional work of teachers. *Educational Psychology Review, 21*(3), 193–218.

Chaplain, R. P. (2008). Stress and psychological distress among trainee secondary teachers in England. *Educational Psychology, 28*(2), 195–209.

Corey, G., Muratori, M., Austin, J. T. I., & Austin, J. A. (2018). Counselor self-care. http://ebookcentral.proquest.com

Costa, A. L., Garmston, R. J., Hayes, C., & Ellison, J. (2016). *Cognitive coaching: Developing self-directed leaders and learners*. Rowman & Littlefield.

Creswell, J. W., & Plano Clark, V. L. (2017). *Designing and conducting mixed methods research* (3rd ed.). SAGE.

Darling-Hammond, L. (2000). *Solving the dilemmas of teacher supply, demand, and quality*. National Commission on Teaching and America's Future.

Delaney, M. (2018). Caring for the caregivers: Evaluation of the effect of an eight-week pilot mindful self-compassion (MSC) training program on nurses' compassion fatigue and resilience. *PLoS ONE, 13*(11), 1–20 https://doi.org/10.1371/journal.pone.0207261

Diliberti, M. K., & Schwartz, H. L. (2023). *Educator turnover has markedly increased, but districts have taken actions to boost teacher ranks: Selected findings from the sixth American school district panel survey*. RAND Corporation. https://www.rand.org/pubs/research_reports/RRA956-14.html

Dingus, J. E. (2008). "I'm learning the trade": Mentoring networks of Black women teachers. *Urban Education, 43*(3), 361–377.

Djonko-Moore, C. M. (2016). An exploration of teacher attrition and mobility in high poverty racially segregated schools. *Race Ethnicity and Education, 19*(5), 1063–1087.

Dreisoerner, A., Junker, N., & van Dick, R. (2020). The relationship among the components of self-compassion: A pilot study using a compassionate writing intervention to enhance self-kindness, common humanity, and mindfulness. *Journal of Happiness Studies, 22*, 21–47. https://doi.org/10.1007/s10902-019-00217-4

Duarte, J., Pinto-Gouveia, J., & Cruz, B. (2016). Relationships between nurses' empathy, self-compassion and dimensions of professional quality of life: A cross-sectional study. *International Journal of Nursing Studies, 60*, 1–11.

Dunn, A. H. (2018). Leaving a profession after it's left you: Teachers' public resignation letters as resistance amidst neoliberalism. *Teachers College Record, 120*(9), 1–34.

Dweck, C. (2012). *Mindset: How you can fulfill your potential.* Robinson Publishing.
Dweck, C. (2014). How can you develop a growth mindset about teaching? *Educational Horizons, 93*(2), 10-15.
Early, D. M., & Winton, P. J. (2001). Preparing the workforce: Early childhood teacher preparation at 2- and 4-year institutions of higher education. *Early Childhood Research Quarterly, 16*(3), 285–306.
Elkind, D. (1967). Egocentrism in adolescence. *Child Development, 38*(4), 1025–1034.
Eriksson, T., Germundsjo, L., Astrom, E., & Ronnlund, M. (2018). Mindful self-compassion training reduces stress and burnout symptoms among practicing psychologists: A randomized controlled trial of a brief web-based intervention. *Frontiers in Psychology, 9,* 1–10.
Facchinetti, A. (2010). Education revolution. *Education Today, 10.*
Fantilli, R. D., & McDougall, D. E. (2009). A study of novice teachers: Challenges and supports in the first years. *Teaching and Teacher Education, 25*(6), 814–825.
Finlay-Jones, A. L., Rees, C. S., & Kane, R. T. (2015). Self-compassion, emotion regulation and stress among Australian psychologists: Testing an emotion regulation model of self-compassion using structural equation modeling. *PLos ONE, 10*(7), e0133481.
Finlay-Jones, A., Xie, Q., Huang, X., Ma, X., & Guo, X. (2017). A pilot study of the 8-week mindful self-compassion training program in a Chinese community sample. *Mindfulness, 9,* 993–1002. https://doi.org/10.1007/s12671-017-0838-3
Franco, C., Mañas, I., Cangas, A. J., Moreno, E., & Gallego, J. (2010). Reducing teachers' psychological distress through a mindfulness training program. *Spanish Journal of Psychology, 13*(2), 655–666.
Gee, J. P. (1996). *Social linguistics and literacies: Ideology in discourses* (2nd ed.). Taylor & Francis.
Germer, C. K., & Neff, K. D. (2017). *Mindful self-compassion handout booklet.* Center for Mindful Self-Compassion.
Gold, Y. (1985). Does teacher burnout begin with student teaching? *Education, 105*(3), 254–257.
Gomez, M. L., & Rodriguez, T. L. (2011, Winter). Imagining the knowledge, strengths, and skills of a Latina prospective teacher. *Teacher Education Quarterly, 38*(1), 127–146.
Graue, M. E., & Walsh, D. J. (1998). *Studying children in context: Theories, methods, and ethics.* SAGE.
Haviland, V. S. (2008). "Things get glossed over": Rearticulating the silencing power of whiteness in education. *Journal of Teacher Education, 59*(1), 40–54.
Hirshberg, M. J. (2017). *Well-being training for preservice teachers* (Publication No. 10622669) [Doctoral dissertation, University of Wisconsin-Madison]. ProQuest Dissertations Publishing.
Horgan, K., Howard, S., & Gardiner-Hyland, F. (2018). Pre-service teachers and stress during microteaching: An experimental investigation of the effectiveness of relaxation training with biofeedback on psychological and physiological indices of stress. *Applied Psychophysiology and Biofeedback, 43*(3), 217–225.
Hwang, Y. -S., Noh, J. -E., Medvedev, O. N., & Singh, N. N. (2019a). Effects of a mindfulness-based program for teachers on teacher wellbeing and person-centered teaching practices. *Mindfulness, 10*(11), 2385–2402.

Hwang, Y. -S., Medvedev, O. N., Krägeloh, C., Hand, K., Noh, J. -E., & Singh, N. N. (2019b). The role of dispositional mindfulness and self-compassion in educator stress. *Mindfulness, 10*(8), 1692–1702.

Ingersoll, R. M. (2001). Teacher turnover and teacher shortages: An organizational analysis. *American Educational Research Journal, 38*(3), 499–534.

Ingersoll, R. M., & Connor, R. (2009, April). *What the national data tell us about minority and Black teacher turnover* [Session presentation]. American Educational Research Association Annual Meeting, San Diego, CA.

Ingersoll, R. M., & Smith, T. M. (2003). The wrong solution to the teacher shortage. *Educational Leadership, 60*(8), 30–33.

Jennings, P. A., Brown, J. L., Frank, J. L., Doyle, S., Oh, Y., Davis, R., Rasheed, D., DeWeese, A., DeMauro, A. A., Cham, H., & Greenberg, M. T. (2017). Impacts of the CARE for Teachers program on teachers' social and emotional competence and classroom interactions. *Journal of Educational Psychology, 109*(7), 1010–1028.

Johnston, P. (2003). *Choice words*. Stenhouse Publishers.

Kabat-Zinn, J. (1994). *Wherever you go, there you are: Mindfulness meditation in everyday life*. Hyperion.

Kelly, A. L., & Berthelsen, D. C. (1995). Preschool teachers' experiences of stress. *Teaching and Teacher Education, 11*(4), 345–357.

Kleickmann, T., Richter, D., Kunter, M., Elsner, J., Besser, M., Krauss, S., & Baumert, J. (2013). Teachers' content knowledge and pedagogical content knowledge: The role of structural differences in teacher education. *Journal of Teacher Education, 64*(1), 90–106.

Knier, S., Watson, J., & Duffy, J. (2020). The effects of mindful self-compassion (MSC) training on increasing self-compassion in healthcare professionals. *The American Journal of Occupational Therapy, 74*(1 supplement).

Kohli, R. (2008, Fall). Breaking the cycle of racism in the classroom: Critical race reflections from future teachers of color. *Teacher Education Quarterly*, 177–178.

Ladson-Billings, G. (1991). Beyond multicultural illiteracy. *Journal of Negro Education, 60*(2), 147–157.

López, A., Sanderman, R., Smink, A., Zhang, Y., van Sonderen, E., Ranchor, A., & Schroevers, M. J. (2015). A reconsideration of the self-compassion scale's total score: Self-compassion versus self-criticism. *PloS One, 10*(7).

Maguire, M. (2001). Bullying and the postgraduate secondary school trainee teacher: An English case study. *Journal of Education for Teaching: International Research and Pedagogy, 27*(1), 95–109.

Maslach, C., & Leiter, M. P. (2016). Understanding the burnout experience: Recent research and its implications for psychiatry. *World Psychiatry, 15*(2), 103–111.

McCann, T. M., & Johannessen, L. R. (2004). Why do new teachers cry? *Clearing House, 77*(4), 138–145.

Merriam, S. B., & Tisdell, E. J. (2016). *Qualitative research: A guide to design and implementation* (4th ed.). Jossey-Bass.

Milner, H. R., & Hoy, A. W. (2003). A case study of an African American Teacher's self-efficacy, stereotype threat, and persistence. *Teaching and Teacher Education, 19*(2), 263–276.

References

Montero-Marin, J., Zubiaga, F., Cereceda, M., Demarzo, M. M. P., Trenc, P., & Garcia-Campayo, J. (2016). Burnout subtypes and absence of self-compassion in primary healthcare professionals: A cross-sectional study. *PLoS ONE, 11*(6), 1–17.

Murray-Harvey, R. T., Slee, P., Lawson, M. J., Silins, H., Banfield, G., & Russell, A. (2000). Under stress: The concerns and coping strategies of teacher education students. *European Journal of Teacher Education, 23*(1), 19–35.

Neff, K. D. (2003). Self-compassion: An alternative conceptualization of a healthy attitude toward oneself. *Self and Identity, 2*(2), 85–102.

Neff, K. D. (2011). *Self-compassion*. William-Morrow.

Neff, K. D., & Germer, C. K. (2013). A pilot study and randomized controlled trial of the mindful self-compassion program. *Journal of Clinical Psychology, 69*(1), 28–44.

Neff, K. D., & Germer, C. K. (2018). *The mindful self-compassion workbook*. Guildford Press.

Neff, K. D., Knox, M. C., Long, P., & Gregory, K. (2020). Caring for others without losing yourself: An adaptation of the mindful self-compassion program for healthcare communities. *Journal of Clinical Psychology, 76*(9), 1543–1562.

Onchwari, J. (2010). Early childhood inservice and preservice teachers' perceived levels of preparedness to handle stress in their students. *Early Childhood Education Journal, 37*(5), 391–400.

Patton, M. Q. (2015). *Qualitative research and evaluation methods* (4th ed.). Sage.

Pintrich, P. R., & Blumenfeld, P. C. (1985). Classroom experience and children's self-perceptions of ability, effort, and conduct. *Journal of Educational Psychology, 77*(6), 646–657.

Raes, F., Pommier, E., Neff, K. D., & Van Gucht, D. (2011). Construction and factorial validation of a short form of the self-compassion scale. *Clinical Psychology & Psychotherapy, 18*(3), 250–255.

Roeser, R. W., Schonert-Reichl, K. A., Jha, A., Cullen, M., Wallace, L., Wilensky, R., Oberle, E., Thomson, K., Taylor, C., & Harrison, J. (2013). Mindfulness training and reductions in teacher stress and burnout: Results from two randomized, waitlist-control field trials. *Journal of Educational Psychology, 105*(3), 787–804.

Ryan, S. V., von der Embse, N. P., Pendergast, L. L., Saeki, E., Segool, N., & Schwing, S. (2017). Leaving the teaching profession: The role of teacher stress and educational accountability policies on turnover intent. *Teaching and Teacher Education, 66*, 1–11.

Shapiro, S. L., Astin, J. A., Bishop, S. R., & Cordova, M. (2005). Mindfulness-based stress reduction for health care professionals: Results from a randomized trial. *International Journal of Stress Management, 12*(2), 164–176.

Sheets, R. H., & Chew, L. (2002). Absent from the research, present in our classrooms: Preparing culturally responsive Chinese American teachers. *Journal of Teacher Education, 53*(2), 127–141.

Shulman, L. S. (1986). Those who understand: Knowledge growth in teaching. *Educational Researcher, 15*(2), 4–14.

Siegel, R. D. (2010). *The mindfulness solution*. Guilford Press.

Simos, M. (2013, March 27). Policies lead to teacher burnout. *The Adelaide Advertiser*, p. 29.

Sinclair, S., Kondejewski, J., Raffin-Bouchal, S., King-Shier, K. M., & Singh, P. (2017). Can self-compassion promote healthcare provider well-being and compassionate care to others? Results of a systematic review. *Applied Psychology: Health and Well-Being, 9*(2), 168–206.

Sleeter, C. E. (2001). Epistemological diversity in research on preservice teacher preparation for historically underserved children. *Review of Research in Education, 25*(1), 209–250.

Stebnicki, M. A. (2015). *The professional counselor's desk reference* (2nd ed.). Springer Publishing.

Su, Z. (1997). Teaching as a profession and as a career: Minority candidates' perspectives. *Teaching and Teacher Education, 13*(3), 325–340.

Thomas, G. (2016). *How to do your case study* (2nd ed.). SAGE.

Villegas, A. M., & Irvine, J. J. (2009, April). *Arguments for increasing the racial/ethnic diversity of the teaching force: A look at the evidence* [Paper presentation]. American Educational Research Conference Annual Meeting, San Diego, CA, United States.

Weisman, E. M., & Hansen, L. E. (2008). Student teaching in urban and suburban schools: Perspectives of Latino preservice teachers. *Urban Education, 43*(6), 653–670.

Westervelt, E. (2016, September 15). Frustration. Burnout. Attrition. It's time to address the national teacher shortage. *NPR Ed*. https://www.npr.org/sections/ed/2016/09/15/493808213/frustration-burnout-attrition-its-time-to-address-the-national-teacher-shortage

Wetzel, M., Hoffman, J., & Maloch, B. (2017). *Mentoring preservice teachers through practice: A framework for coaching with CARE*. Routledge.

Wong, C., & Mak, S. (2016). Writing can heal: Effects of self-compassion writing among Hong Kong Chinese college students. *Asian American Journal of Psychology, 7*(1), 74–82.

Wrobel, M. (2013). Can empathy lead to emotional exhaustion in teachers? The mediating role of emotional labor. *International Journal of Occupational Medicine and Environmental Health, 26*(4), 581–592.

Yarnell, L. M., Stafford, R. E., Neff, K. D., Reilly, E. D., Knox, M. C., & Mullarkey, M. (2015). Meta-analysis of gender differences in self-compassion. *Self and Identity, 14*(5), 499–520.

Yela, J., Gomez-Martinez, M., Crego, A., & Jimenez, L. (2019). Effects of the mindful self-compassion programme on clinical and health psychology trainees' well-being: A pilot study. *Clinical Psychologist, 2*(4), 42–54.

Yong, Z., & Yue, Y. (2007). Causes for burnout among secondary and elementary school teachers and preventive strategies. *Chinese Education and Society, 40*(5), 78–85.

Zimmermann, L., Wangler, J., Unterbrink, T., Pfeifer, R., Wirsching, M., & Bauer, J. (2008). Mental health in a German teacher sample at the beginning of their occupational career. *International Journal of Psychology, 43*(3-4), 483–483.

Index

Abenavoli, R. M., 13, 30
Academic content
  stress of delivering to students, 56–78
Achinstein, B., 52
Adams, R., 47, 130
Administrators, relationship dynamics with other teachers and, 104–106
Amos, Y. T., 11, 12, 13, 18, 50, 51, 52, 53
Amrani, P., 18
Astin, J. A., 6, 7, 17, 78

Barnard, L. K., 6, 7, 17, 28, 34, 53, 54, 78, 129
Barry, D. P., 4, 5, 6, 7, 13, 16, 17, 18, 19, 29, 58, 75, 76, 78, 90, 131
Behavioral needs, of students
  stress of meeting, 79–56
Beltman, S., 4, 12, 128, 129, 130
Benzo, R. P., 18, 25
Bishop, S. R., 6, 7, 17, 78
Blumenfeld, P. C., 69, 70
Burnout, 8–9
  self-compassion and, 29–31, 45–48

Cannon, W. B., 84
Chang, M. L., 10, 18, 47, 128
Chew, L., 11, 12, 50, 53
Classroom communities, self-compassion and, 48–50
Cohort coordinators
  impressions of self-compassion, 45–50
Color, preservice teachers of, 11–12
Common humanity, 16
Content knowledge
  insufficient, 61–62
  pedagogical, 61–62

Cooperating teachers,
  relationship dynamics with, 98–103
Cordova, M., 6, 7, 17, 78
Crego, A., 18, 28, 34, 54, 129
Curry, J. F., 6, 7, 17, 28, 34, 53, 54, 78, 129

Darling-Hammond, L., 2, 3, 10, 56, 59, 133
Data
  analysis, 26–27
  sources and collection, 25–26
Djonko-Moore, C. M., 3, 9, 11, 17, 130
Duffy, J., 18, 28, 34, 54, 129

Early childhood stakeholders
  policymakers, 130–131
  teacher educators, 131–133
Emotional needs, of students
  stress of meeting, 79–56
Exploring Self-Compassion Through Letter Writing, 19–21

Field supervisors
  impressions of self-compassion, 45–50
Freitas, C., 52

Gomez-Martinez, M., 18, 28, 34, 54, 129
Greenberg, M. T., 13, 30

Hansen, L. E., 11, 12, 50, 51, 53
Harris, A. R., 13, 30
Hoffman, J., 102, 103, 113, 131

Hoy, A. W., 21
Humanity, common, 16

Ideas, development of, 62–64
Identity, racial
  impact on preservice teachers, 50–53
Irvine, J. J., 52

Jennings, P. A., 13, 30
Jimenez, L., 18, 28, 34, 54, 129
Johannessen, L. R., 10, 59

Katz, D. A., 13, 30
King-Shier, K. M., 17, 18
Kirsch, J. L., 18, 25
Knier, S., 18, 28, 34, 54, 129
Knox, M. C., 24, 129
Kohli, R., 11, 50, 53
Kondejewski, J., 17, 18

Ladson-Billings, G., 11, 52
Leiter, M. P., 18, 128

Maguire, M., 10
Mak, S., 20, 24, 129
Maloch, B., 102, 103, 113, 131
Mansfield, C., 4, 12, 128, 129, 130
Maslach, C., 18, 128
McCann, T. M., 10, 59
Merriam, S. B., 22, 24, 26, 27, 28, 29
Milner, H. R., 21
Mindfulness, 15
  interventions based on, 17–19
Mindful Self-Compassion Program (MSC), 18
Mixed-methods case study, 22–55
  data analysis, 26–27
  data sources and collection, 24–26
  participant identities, 23–24
  trustworthiness, 27–28
Mullarkey, M., 24, 129

Neff, K. D., 5, 6, 7, 9, 14, 15, 16, 17, 18, 19, 20, 21, 22, 23, 24, 25, 26, 28, 31, 32, 34, 39, 40, 41, 44, 47, 48, 53, 54, 55, 58, 68, 70, 71, 72, 73, 74, 75, 76, 91, 92, 93, 94, 112, 113, 114, 117, 123, 124, 125, 129, 132, 135
Nelson, C., 18, 25

Ogawa, R. T., 52
Onchwari, J., 10, 59, 63, 64, 65, 68, 84, 88, 91, 131

Paired sample T-tests, 142
Parents, students, relationship dynamics with, 107–108
Patton, M. Q., 27
Pedagogical content knowledge (PCK), 61–62
Pendergast, L. L., 3, 9, 17, 30, 40, 46, 47, 128, 130
Pintrich, P. R., 69, 70
Policymakers, 130–131
Pommier, E., 6, 23, 24, 26, 28, 53, 55, 58, 129, 135
Preservice teachers
  of color, 11–12
  experiences with stress, 10–12
  impact of identity, 50–53
  and mixed-methods case study.
    See Mixed-methods case study
  self-compassion and, 17, 19–21
  self-compassionate letter-writing practice, 28–36
  stress among. See Stress, preservice teachers
  stress of life outside classroom.
    See Stress of life outside classroom
  well-being, scholarship aimed at addressing, 12–14
Price, A., 4, 12, 128, 129, 130

Qualitative data, mixed-methods case study
  data analysis, 26–27
  data sources and collection, 25–26
Quantitative data, mixed-methods case study
  data analysis, 26
  data sources and collection, 24–25
Questions, development of, 62–64

Index

Racial identity
 impact on preservice teachers, 50–53
Raes, F., 6, 23, 24, 26, 28, 53, 55, 58, 129, 135
Raffin-Bouchal, S., 17, 18
Reilly, E. D., 24, 129
Relationship dynamics
 with cooperating teachers, 98–103
 with other teachers and administrators, 104–106
 with students' parents, 107–108
 with teacher educators, 108–111
Resident assistant (RA), 119
Role conflict, students' challenging behavior with, 84–85
Ryan, S. V., 3, 9, 17, 30, 40, 46, 47, 128, 130

Saeki, E., 3, 9, 17, 30, 40, 46, 47, 128, 130
Schwing, S., 3, 9, 17, 30, 40, 46, 47, 128, 130
Segool, N., 3, 9, 17, 30, 40, 46, 47, 128, 130
Self-care vs. self-compassion, 16–17
Self-compassion, 111–118
 and burnout, 29–31, 45–48
 classroom communities and, 48–50
 components of, 15–16
 defined, 14
 field supervisors and cohort coordinators' impressions of, 45–50
 misconceptions of, 16
 past, present, and future, 36–44
 scale statistical analysis, 53
 self-care vs., 16–17
 and stress, 29–31, 45–48
 and teachers/preservice teachers, 17, 19–21
Self-Compassion (Neff), 19
Self-compassionate letters, 68–78
 addressing stress of managing relationship dynamics with cooperating teachers, 113–115
 addressing stress of meeting students' social, emotional, and behavioral needs, 90–96
 educators', 112–113
 example of, 115–116
 significance of, 129
 writing, addressing stress of managing relationship dynamics with families, 116–118
 writing practice, 28–36
Self-Compassion Scale: Short Form (Neff), 135–136
 data sources and collection, 24–25
 descriptive statistics of, 137–141
 paired sample T-tests, 142
 quantitative analysis of, 26
Self-kindness, 15
Sexton, D., 52
Shapiro, S. L., 6, 7, 17, 78
Sheets, R. H., 11, 12, 50, 53
Shulman, L. S., 61, 62, 63, 66, 69, 74
Siegel, R. D., 41, 70, 71, 72, 91, 92, 123
Simos, M., 47, 130
Sinclair, S., 17, 18
Singh, P., 17, 18
Sleeter, C. E., 11, 52
Social–emotional learning (SEL), 109
Social needs, of students
 stress of meeting, 79–56
Stafford, R. E., 24, 129
Stebnicki, M. A., 18, 28, 34, 54, 129
Stress, preservice teachers, 10–12
 delivering academic content to students, 56–78
 meeting students' social, emotional, and behavioral needs, 79–96
 relationship dynamics with cooperating teachers, school staff, families, and teacher educators, 97–127
 scholarly attempts at reducing, 17–21
 self-compassion and, 29–31, 45–48
Stress of life outside classroom, 119–127
 addressing with self-compassion, 122–127
 balancing life, need for, 120–122

Students
  developing relationships with, 92–93
  parents, relationship dynamics with, 107–108
  stress of delivering academic content to, 56–78
  stress of meeting, social, emotional, and behavioral needs, 79–96
Su, Z., 52

Teacher educators, 131–133
  relationship dynamics with, 108–111
Teachers, preservice. *See* Preservice teachers
Thomas, G., 28
Tisdell, E. J., 22, 24, 26, 27, 28, 29
Trustworthiness, 27–28

Van Gucht, D., 6, 23, 24, 26, 28, 53, 55, 58, 129, 135
Villegas, A. M., 52
von der Embse, N. P., 3, 9, 17, 30, 40, 46, 47, 128, 130

Watson, J., 18, 28, 34, 54, 129
Weisman, E. M., 11, 12, 50, 51, 53
Westervelt, E., 9, 30
Wetzel, M., 102, 103, 113, 131
Whiteness, 11–12
Wong, C., 20, 24, 129
Wrobel, M., 10, 13, 30

Yarnell, L. M., 24, 129
Yela, J., 18, 28, 34, 54, 129
Yong, Z., 10, 47, 107, 108, 116, 130
Yue, Y., 10, 47, 107, 108, 116, 130

About the Author

David (Dave) P. Barry is an assistant professor of early childhood education at West Chester University of Pennsylvania. He was a pre-K and kindergarten teacher for over 10 years, and his research interests center on early childhood teachers' well-being at every career stage. He has personally experienced the power of self-compassion to address the stressors of teaching young children and believes wholeheartedly that attending to teachers' well-being will inevitably impact students' well-being and achievement.